THE MAN FROM OUTSIDE

THE MAN FROM OUTSIDE

by

GORDON BRIDGER

Chaplain, St Thomas's Church, Edinburgh

INTER-VARSITY PRESS

INTER-VARSITY PRESS

Inter-Varsity Fellowship
39 Bedford Square, London WC1

Inter-Varsity Christian Fellowship
130 north Wells, Chicago, Illinois 60606

© INTER-VARSITY PRESS, LONDON
First Edition March 1969

UK STANDARD BOOK NUMBER 85110 343 X

Printed in Great Britain by
Hazell Watson & Viney Ltd., Aylesbury, Bucks

CONTENTS

INTRODUCTION

I HAD BEEN speaking to some students about the claims of Jesus Christ and of Christianity. A friend of mine passed on to me afterwards the comment of an interested but uncommitted fellow-student who had heard the talk. It was something like this: 'I wish he hadn't assumed that we all believe the Bible is true.'

I do not want to assume this in introducing John's Gospel. There is certainly not space to outline all the reasons for my personal conviction that the Bible is reliable. Some who read this will already be convinced. Others will not. But I want to suggest some reasons for believing that in reading this part of the New Testament we are considering an important and trustworthy source-book of Christianity. We are looking at a contemporary account of the most exciting and astonishing events of all time, events that centred on a unique person, Jesus of Nazareth.

Dorothy Sayers once deplored the fact that so many people appeared to regard the events and dogmas of the New Testament as dull. She wrote: 'Here we had a man of divine character walking and talking among us—and what did we find to do with Him? The common people, indeed, "heard Him gladly". But our leading authorities in Church and State considered that He talked too much and uttered too many disconcerting truths. So we bribed one of His friends to hand Him over quietly to the police, and we tried Him on a rather vague charge of creating a disturbance, and had Him publicly hanged on the common gallows, "thanking God we were rid of a knave". All this was not very creditable to us, even if He was (as many people thought and think) only a harmless, crazy preacher. But if the Church is right about Him, it was more discreditable still, for the Man we hanged was God Almighty. . . . This is the dogma we find so dull—the terrifying drama of which

God is the victim and hero. If this is dull, then what in Heaven's name is worthy to be called exciting!'*

This Gospel, then, is the story of the Man from Outside—the man from outside our own experience, outside, as we shall see, anything the world had known before. He was very much an outsider, too, with the Establishment of his time, so much so that it was the religious leaders who hounded him to death. But before we plunge into the story, we must first clear the ground. How can we be reasonably sure that John gives us a reliable account of these exciting events?

a. The reliability of John's Gospel

1. *Are the documents reliable?* There is much more evidence for the reliability of the New Testament documents than for any other writings of comparable date.† No classical scholar would deny that Thucydides and Tacitus wrote their histories. Yet the earliest manuscript we have of Thucydides' work is dated well over a thousand years after he wrote; and the manuscript for Tacitus is dated 800 years later. On the other hand, we have two complete New Testaments dated little more than 300 years after the originals;‡ a papyrus copy of about three-quarters of the New Testament about 200 years after the events,§ which includes sections of John's Gospel; the recently-discovered Bodmer papyrus which contains most of John's Gospel (dated about AD 200); and the famous John Rylands fragment, now in Manchester, but found in Egypt, and dated between AD 117 and 138. This must have been circulating within forty years of the writing of John's Gospel.

We may add to the weight of this documentary evidence the frequent quotations from the Gospels in various second-century works. So by comparing the various documents it is possible to arrive at a firm conclusion about the accuracy of copying, and the extent of alterations in the text. On the basis of such evidence a scholar of the standing of the late Sir Frederic Kenyon of the

* Dorothy Sayers, *Creed and Chaos*, p. 3.
† Read F. F. Bruce, *The New Testament Documents* for a fuller treatment of this subject.
‡ Codex Vaticanus and Codex Sinaiticus. The former is in the Vatican Library and the latter in the British Museum. § Chester Beatty Papyri.

British Museum could say: 'Both the authenticity and the general integrity of the books of the New Testament may be regarded as finally established.'*

'Very well,' you will say, 'but even if the documents are reliable, we may still be reading fiction rather than fact. How can we be sure that Jesus was real rather than legendary?'

2. *Is Jesus a historical person?* If we read the Gospels with an open mind, we may decide for ourselves whether there is a self-evident truthfulness about the stories.† Certainly it is hard to imagine why the writers of the New Testament should make up such a story, and in some cases die for it, if they knew it was not true. Furthermore, there is a ring of truth about the story of Jesus in the Gospels which is not echoed in later non-apostolic writings. In the so-called *Gospel of Thomas*, for example, we find this: 'The little child Jesus, when he was five years old, was playing at the ford of a brook. And having made soft clay he fashioned thereof 12 sparrows. And it was the sabbath day when he did these things. And Joseph came to the place and cried out to him saying: "Wherefore doest thou these things on the sabbath which it is not lawful to do?" But Jesus clapped his hands together, and said to them "Go!" And the sparrows took their flight and went away chirping.' The Jesus of the New Testament is not a magician like the apocryphal Jesus.

If, however, the internal evidence of the Gospels themselves does not convince us of the reality of a Jesus of history, there is external evidence to be considered. The Roman historian Tacitus lived between AD 60 and 120. When referring to the fire of Rome and the Neronian persecution, he wrote (*c.* AD 100): 'Nero set up as the culprits and punished with the utmost refinements of cruelty a class hated for their abominations . . . who are commonly called Christians. Christus, from whom their name is derived, was executed at the hands of the procurator Pontius Pilate in the reign of Tiberius.'‡ We might have expected that the execution of a

* F. G. Kenyon, *The Bible and Archaeology*, p. 288.
† J. B. Phillips, *Ring of Truth* is an interesting testimony of a famous translator of the Bible to this conviction. See also Michael Green, *Runaway World*, especially the first chapter on 'Running away from history'.
‡ Tacitus, *Annales*, xv. 44.

village carpenter, occurring in a completely obscure province, with the minimum of publicity, would have been forgotten in a week. Yet a generation later Rome is resounding with the news of it.

Another example is that of Suetonius, who refers (*c.* AD 120) to the expulsion of the Jews from Rome in AD 49 through quarrelling over one 'Chrestus'.* The governor of Bithynia, Pliny the younger, writing around AD 110, refers to the Christians who meet in his province and gather every morning to sing a hymn to Christ as God.†

One further quotation must suffice. The writer was a contemporary of John, but he was not a Christian. 'About this time lived Jesus, a man full of wisdom, if one may call him a man. For he was the doer of incredible things, and the teacher of such as gladly accepted the truth. He thus attracted to himself many Jews and many of the Gentiles. He was the Christ. On the accusation of the leading men of our people, Pilate condemned him to death upon the cross. Nevertheless those who had previously loved him still remained faithful to him. On the third day he again appeared to them living, just as, in addition to a thousand other wonderful things, prophets sent by God had foretold. And at the present day the race of those who call themselves Christians after him has not ceased.'‡ The writer was Josephus, a Jewish historian, writing at the end of the first century AD. We need have no doubt that Jesus really lived.

But this leads to a further question about John's Gospel itself.

3. *Is John's Gospel accurate?* It is not difficult to see that John's Gospel is different from those of Matthew, Mark and Luke (often called the Synoptic Gospels) in a number of ways. If we had only John's Gospel as a record of the life and ministry of Jesus Christ we should be ignorant of such important features as the birth and childhood of Jesus, and the Last Supper. We should know nothing of His teaching by parables, His healing of lepers and demoniacs, or His association with those highly unpopular civil servants, the tax-collectors. We should know nothing of the Lord's Prayer.

* Suetonius, *Life of Claudius*, 25.
† Pliny, *Letters*, x.
‡ Josephus, *Antiquities of the Jews*, xviii. 3. 3.

On the other hand, John's Gospel alone tells us a great deal that we would not glean from the Synoptics. John alone tells us that Jesus frequently visited Jerusalem, though the Synoptics hint at this in the prayer of Jesus for Jerusalem: 'O Jerusalem, Jerusalem, killing the prophets and stoning those who are sent to you! *How often* would I have gathered your children together as a hen gathers her brood under her wings, and you would not!' (Luke 13:34; Matthew 23:37–39). John alone tells us in any detail about the Judean ministry of Jesus. He alone writes about the wedding reception in Cana, the interviews with Nicodemus and the Samaritan woman, the raising of Lazarus from the dead and certain teaching about the Holy Spirit.

Another difference between John's Gospel and the Synoptics is the different style in the teaching of Jesus. It was fashionable, therefore, some years ago to dismiss John's Gospel as of doubtful historical value. John, it was agreed, was more concerned with theology than with history. Certain terms, such as 'the Word' or 'Logos' (John 1:1), 'children of light' and 'walking in darkness', were supposed to be more suitable for a late-second-century gnostic philosopher than for a first-century fisherman. Furthermore, it was believed that John was hopelessly inaccurate on his topography and knowledge of south Palestinian life, and that some of the places he mentions were obviously a figment of the author's imagination.

In recent years a number of discoveries and a reconsideration of this Gospel have tended to confirm more and more its historical as well as theological value, and its accuracy. It is now generally believed that John wrote independently of the sources of the Synoptics, though no doubt he had knowledge of them; and it may well be that he wrote deliberately to supplement the teaching of the Synoptics.* He wrote for a definite purpose (see 20:31), and he was selective in his use of material. The style of teaching in his Gospel may well reflect his manner of debate with the Rabbis in Jerusalem; for there seems to be little doubt that the Rabbis had a style of their own. No doubt the style is 'Radio 3' rather than 'Radio 1' or '2';

* For a fuller discussion of the relationship between John's Gospel and the Synoptics read the Introduction by R. V. G. Tasker in *The Gospel according to St. John (Tyndale New Testament Commentaries)*.

but there is no reason to believe that Jesus would not adapt Himself to the people to whom He was speaking. We now know, from the recent discovery of the Dead Sea Scrolls, that phrases used in John's Gospel such as 'children of light', 'life eternal', 'Spirit of truth', 'walking in the light', 'walking in the darkness', 'the light of life', do not indicate that the Gospel must have been written in the second century. These phrases can all be found in the Qumran text which is dated *before* the time of Jesus Christ.

Most interesting of all have been the archaeological discoveries that have certainly tended to confirm the accuracy of John's Gospel. The Pool of Bethesda, for example, was once thought to be non-existent as there was no trace of it in ancient literature or through archaeological excavations. Now this pool has been discovered, and the name is referred to in one of the Dead Sea Scrolls! Votive inscriptions indicate that the water was believed to possess healing properties. The Pool of Siloam is another exciting archaeological find. Gabbatha, 'the place of the pavement' (19:13), was once dismissed as unhistorical. In 1934 Père Vincent, excavating in Jerusalem, discovered it some 20 feet below the surface of the city. It is 50 yards square, and was part of the Roman barracks destroyed before AD 70. The pavement can be seen in Jerusalem today.

Again, even the place-names in John's Gospel, and some of the names of people such as Lazarus and Martha, were once thought to be profoundly symbolical and highly fanciful. Some of the names of people have now turned up on ossuary inscriptions at a date which confirms John's use of them. Archaeology has also shown that many of the place-names John uses are far from fictitious and belong to early tradition stemming from the period before the destruction of Jerusalem in AD 70. In John 3:23, for example, John the Baptist is said to have been baptizing 'at Aenon near Salim, because there was much water there'. Salim has now been identified with a town of this name south east of Nablus, and Aenon with the neighbouring modern Aenum. This district abounds in springs. A recent writer,* after a careful reading of John 4:46–54, described his own conviction that John must have been very familiar with the topography of that part of Palestine. 'There is a marked stress

* R. D. Potter, *Studia Evangelica*, p. 329.

on the descent from Cana to Capernaum—the author knew and felt the drop from well above sea-level to well below sea-level, which is so marked a feature of that region then as nowadays.'* The accuracy of John's Gospel continues to be confirmed by modern scholarship.

b. The authorship and date of John's Gospel

This Gospel has been called the Gospel *according to John* since the second century. The traditional view of the Christian church has been that this John is the apostle John, the son of Zebedee, a Galilaean fisherman in partnership with James and Peter (Luke 5:7–10). He was one of the twelve disciples of Jesus, an eyewitness of His life, death and resurrection.

There is considerable external evidence to support John's close association with this Gospel. Irenaeus, who became Bishop of Lyons in AD 177, wrote: 'John, the disciple of the Lord, who also leant upon His heart, himself also published the gospel in Ephesus when he was living in Asia.' Clement of Alexandria wrote (*c.* AD 230): 'Last of all, John, perceiving that the bodily facts had been made plain in the gospel, being urged by his friends composed a spiritual gospel.' Perhaps the most important document is the Muratorian Canon compiled in Rome *c.* AD 170. This manuscript includes this comment: 'At the request of his fellow disciples and of his bishops, John, one of the disciples, said, "Fast with me for three days from this time and whatsoever shall be revealed to each of us, whether it be favourable to my writing or not, let us relate it to one another." On the same night it was revealed to Andrew that John should relate all things, aided by the revision of all.'

According to these traditions and others, John the apostle was certainly the authority behind the Gospel. It is not clear whether he wrote every word himself. He could have dictated it to a disciple or disciples who acted as secretaries.

The possibility that John used an amanuensis or secretary is suggested by a consideration of the Gospel itself. John never mentions his own name; but he does refer on several occasions to 'the

---

* For further reading on this subject, see R. D. Harrison, *Archaeology of the New Testament.*

13

disciple whom Jesus loved' (13:23–25; 19:26, 27; 20:2; 21:20) who is probably to be identified with John the son of Zebedee. But it is also possible that there is another disciple who is witnessing to the facts he describes (see John 19:34, 35; 21:24), and who may be actually writing them down.* Some have thought that it is more likely that another man would describe John as 'the disciple whom Jesus loved' than John himself. Whether we allow an amanuensis or not, the internal and external evidence is strongly in favour of the apostolic authority of John as the witness to the life of Christ.

It has sometimes been argued that a Gospel of this kind could not have been written by a Galilaean fisherman. But as someone once commented: 'This might have been said about Ernest Bevin's speeches as Foreign Secretary, "These couldn't have been written by a barrow-boy in east Bristol." To which of course the answer is that they weren't, they were written by a man who *had been* a barrow-boy in east Bristol.'

If, as we believe, John Zebedee is the authority behind this Gospel, then we may confidently date the Gospel around AD 90 to 100. For it is the last Gospel to be written according to the majority of manuscripts; and we know from a strong tradition that John lived to be a very old man into the reign of Trajan, which began in AD 98. The evidence from the Dead Sea Scrolls and the John Rylands fragment rules out the possibility of a late-second-century date for this Gospel.

c. The purpose of the Gospel

What then is the purpose of John's Gospel? John clearly expresses it when he writes (20: 30, 31): 'Now Jesus did many other signs in the presence of the disciples, which are not written in this book; but these are written that you may believe that Jesus is the Christ, the Son of God, and that believing you may have life in his name.'

John undoubtedly writes primarily for those not yet committed to belief in Jesus Christ. One commentator on this Gospel† has

* For a fuller discussion see R. V. G. Tasker, *The Gospel according to St. John.*

† C. H. Dodd, *The Interpretation of the Fourth Gospel.*

14

written: 'The Gospel could be read intelligently by a person who started with no knowledge of Christianity beyond the minimum that a reasonably well informed member of the public interested in religion might be supposed to have by the close of the first century . . . If he was then led to associate himself with the Church . . . he would be able to re-read the book and find in it vastly more than had been obvious at a first reading . . .'

Probably those who read it first would have been Jews, especially those displaced persons scattered through Asia who were influenced to some extent by Greek thought and culture. So John writes that they may come to believe that Jesus is the Messiah, the Anointed One promised to the Jewish people by God through their prophets, as well as the unique Son of God, or God become man. It is clear too that John is writing for those outside Palestine, without much knowledge of Jewish customs. For he has to explain terms such as purification (2:6), burial (19:40), and even such simple Semitic words as Rabbi (1:38) and Rabboni (20:16). Also, Christians did and do find their faith strengthened as they read this Gospel, and chapters 13 to 17 are perhaps especially relevant for already committed Christians.

The teaching of this Gospel would also be specially relevant in combating certain gnostic heresies which denied, for example, the real humanity of Jesus Christ. The humanity of Jesus is emphasized as well as His deity in this Gospel (see 4:6; 9:6; 11:35; 12:27; 19:28, 34). There are sects today, such as Jehovah's Witnesses, Christian Science and Mormonism, who need a similar corrective concerning the person of Christ.

Primarily, however, this Gospel is written to help an individual to a personal faith in Jesus Christ. I remember once talking to a university professor who said rather wistfully, 'How do you woo faith?' John's answer would be: read this account, consider this evidence, consider Jesus. 'These things are written *that you may believe.*' For this Gospel is written to bring before us certain 'signs' and evidences which John has selected (see 20:30, 31) in order that we may believe in Jesus as the Christ and the Son of God, and that believing we may have life in His name.

There are two further questions that we may be asking, even if we are persuaded that John's Gospel is a reliable historical document, and we ourselves are seekers after truth and 'life'.

1. *Why should we read John's Gospel?* A man once said to me that he wanted to read about all the religions of the world before he could decide whether Christianity was true or not. I suggested that he narrowed his search to consider Jesus Christ first, for Jesus made claims for Himself which no other religious leader has ever made. John's Gospel tells us what those claims are, and gives reasons for believing them. If these claims are false, then we are free to consider the merits of other religions. If they are true, they make such total demands upon us that whatever true things may be found in other religions, Christianity must still be uniquely true, and Jesus Christ the only true way to God. As Jesus Himself says, 'I am the way, and the truth, and the life; no one comes to the Father, but by me' (John 14:6). That is either intolerant humbug, or one of the most important statements of all time. We should read John's Gospel, therefore, to find out whether these unique claims of Jesus Christ are true or not.

John's Gospel also claims that believing in Jesus leads to '*life* in his name'. 'Eternal life' is much more than 'living for ever'. It clearly refers to a quality of life here and now which, it is claimed, Jesus gives to those who believe in Him. According to John's Gospel, 'real life', as compared to 'existence', is found only by those who know God and the Lord Jesus Christ (17:3). Men and women are searching for satisfaction now as they were in the first century. Bertrand Russell once said, 'Life is one long second-best.' A current song-writer expresses the same pessimism when he writes, 'I can't get no satisfaction . . . I've tried and I've tried.' Yet the former England and Sussex cricketer, David Sheppard, can write of his own commitment to Jesus Christ and the cricketing career he relinquished, by saying: 'As with so many things in the Christian life, it has not so much been a case of "giving it up", as "taking up" something else which is infinitely worthwhile.'* What was 'infinitely worthwhile' was the new life in Jesus Christ which has eventually led him and his wife to serve God in London's dockland. If the reader is searching for a satisfying and demanding

* D. S. Sheppard, *Parson's Pitch*, p. 245.

life, as well as a life that continues beyond the grave, then John's Gospel claims to show us how this may become ours. That is why we should read it.

2. *How should we read it?* The story is told of the late Dr. Benjamin Jowett, at one time the Master of Balliol College, Oxford, who was not only a great scholar but also a great wit. At dinner one day a lady tried to draw some clever response from him: 'Dr. Jowett, we would like to know what is your opinion of God?' The Master immediately looked stern, and he said, 'Madam, I should think it a great impertinence were I to express my opinion about God. The only constant anxiety of my life is to know what is God's opinion of me.'

It is because John's Gospel claims to tell us, amongst other things, 'God's opinion' of us, that we should read it in the following ways.

Honestly and humbly. More than one person has read John's Gospel with the sincere prayer on their lips, 'O God, if there be a God, reveal yourself to me.' According to the Bible God made this promise to the Jewish people: 'You will seek me and find me; when you seek me *with all your heart*, I will be found by you, says the Lord' (Jeremiah 29:13, 14). In any subject, if we want to find the truth we have to be honest and wholehearted. This is precisely the same when we seek for the truth about God. We shall see in this Gospel that Jesus had nothing to say to triflers. But He once said, 'Seek, and you will find' (Matthew 7:7).

Thoughtfully and regularly. It is possible to read John's Gospel at a sitting, and it is certainly good to do this some time if we can. But this short commentary is designed to encourage you to read about a half a chapter a day. *It is hoped that you will read the passage through at least twice, and think about it, before you read the comments*. The commentary is written only to supplement or reinforce what you may have already discovered.

Practically and obediently. A member of our congregation, now a school-teacher, has told me how she began to read John's Gospel at a time when she had doubts 'whether there could be a God, and even more doubts as to whether Jesus could be God'. She said that she began to read the Gospel in 'fairly large chunks' at night before sleeping. As she finished the closing chapters she remembers telling herself 'it couldn't be otherwise'. Then she added, 'From that time on I was sure there was a God, *although it was years later than I came to trust Christ with my life.*' When John talks about belief in Jesus Christ he means more than intellectual assent to certain facts about Him. He means practical, obedient trust in Him. When we discover truth we must do something about it, if we are not to spend years of our life in uncertainty.

It is my prayer that you will discover and act upon the truth of John's words: 'These things are written that you may believe . . ., and that believing you may have life in his name.'

1 GOD SPEAKS TO MAN

1 In the beginning was the Word, and the Word was with God, and the Word was God. ²He was in the beginning with God; ³all things were made through him, and without him was not anything made that was made. ⁴In him was life, and the life was the light of men. ⁵The light shines in the darkness, and the darkness has not overcome it.

6 There was a man sent from God, whose name was John. ⁷He came for testimony, to bear witness to the light, that all might believe through him. ⁸He was not the light, but came to bear witness to the light.

9 The true light that enlightens every man was coming into the world. ¹⁰He was in the world, and the world was made through him, yet the world knew him not. ¹¹He came to his own home, and his own people received him not. ¹²But to all who received him, who believed in his name, he gave power to become children of God; ¹³who were born, not of blood nor of the will of the flesh nor of the will of man, but of God.

14 And the Word became flesh and dwelt among us, full of grace and truth; we have beheld his glory, glory as of the only Son from the Father. ¹⁵(John bore witness to him, and cried, 'This was he of whom I said, "He who comes after me ranks before me, for he was before me." ')

16 And from his fullness have we all received, grace upon grace. ¹⁷For the law was given through Moses; grace and truth came through Jesus Christ. ¹⁸No one has ever seen God; the only Son, who is in the bosom of the Father, he has made him known.

'Man seeking God', the title given to a BBC series of talks on world religions, sums up many people's definition of 'religion'. The writer of this Gospel makes a more significant claim for Christianity. At this point John does not argue the case, he simply states it. In Jesus, *God is seeking man*. John emphasizes this in three ways.

a. God speaks through Jesus, who is 'the Word'

'In the beginning was the Word.' We should not find it difficult to understand this description of Jesus as 'the Word'. We recognize that it is impossible to get to know a person unless he chooses to speak to us. So man, the creature, cannot expect to know God, the Creator, unless God chooses to speak. That is precisely what God has done. 'At the beginning God expressed himself' is J. B. Phillips' translation of the opening phrase; and the claim of this Gospel is that God has expressed Himself most clearly in Jesus Christ.

The orthodox Jew, like John, would understand this concept of 'the Word' in a deeper sense. The Word of God had come to the Jews through the Law and the Prophets. But now, John claimed, God was speaking with love and truth in a supreme and final way through Jesus Christ (verse 17).

The intelligent Greek reader of John's Gospel would have another thought. For him 'the Word' or 'Logos' (the Greek word that John uses) was the Intelligence behind the universe and the marvels of creation. John claims that Jesus, the Word, *was* that Intelligence. He is the Creator and Sustainer of all things (verses 1–3). Nothing could be clearer in these verses than that John claims that Jesus is the Creator God, and that in Jesus God has spoken His supreme word to man.

I once failed to hear an important party political broadcast. It was not that the Prime Minister failed to speak, but that I failed to tune in. So it is that we sometimes fail to know God, not because He has not spoken, but because we are not tuned in to hear Him.

b. God reveals Himself through Jesus, who is the light

According to the Bible, a man who does not know God is like a man who is walking in the dark. He is ignorant of God. He has lost his way. A. E. Housman expressed the lostness and aimlessness of twentieth-century man when he wrote:

> 'The sun is up and up must I,
> To wash and dress
> And eat and drink

And look at things
And talk and think
And work . . .
And God knows why.'

But God has never left man in total darkness to drift aimlessly along. Jesus, the Word, is also 'the true light that enlightens every man . . .' (verse 9). Even those who have never heard of Christ have seen something of His light in creation.* As that great Christian missionary, the apostle Paul, once wrote: 'Ever since the creation of the world his (God's) invisible nature, namely, his eternal power and deity, has been clearly perceived in the things that have been made' (Romans 1:20).

If Jesus is 'the light that enlightens every man', it is clear too that all men may know something about God in their nature and conscience. God is the Creator of all men (verse 3), and in man's awareness of right and wrong, as well as in his appreciation of all that is good, beautiful and true, Christ may make Himself known. The light shines, and has always shone, in the darkness, and the darkness has never completely overcome it (verse 5).

However, John's most astonishing claim is that God revealed Himself to man in human terms when 'the Word became flesh and dwelt among us, full of grace and truth' (verse 14). This is the light that shines most brightly in the darkness. Not all accepted Jesus or recognized that He was God become man (verse 11). But those who did saw someone who expressed love and truth and 'glory', that is the very presence and power of God. In Jesus, as John the Baptist and John the Evangelist believed, the Invisible God had become visible to man (verse 18). God had come into focus.

Does God seem out of focus, a shadowy, unreal power, an impersonal force? John claims that God has revealed Himself to men in personal, flesh-and-blood terms in Jesus Christ. Here he makes the claim. Later he gives his reasons.

* Cicero once wrote: 'If a man enters a house or a gymnasium of a forum and sees reason, method and discipline reigning there, he cannot suppose that these came about without a cause, but perceives that there is someone there who rules and is obeyed: how much more when he contemplates the motions and revolutions to be seen in the universe (*e.g.* in the heavenly bodies) must he conclude they are all governed by a Conscious Hand.'

c. God gives through Jesus, who is the life

'But to all who received him, . . . he *gave* power' (verse 12); 'And from his fullness have we all *received*' (verse 16). It is not enough to know what God is like. Modern man is not interested in theories about God. He is searching for satisfaction, for 'kicks', for 'experiences', for what he calls 'life'. John claims with other Christians (notice 'we' in verses 14, 16) that it is possible to experience the life of God when we receive Christ, become His children (verse 12) and continue to receive His gifts (verse 16). This 'life' is not to be confused with physical life. Neither does it follow automatically upon physical birth. It is not dependent upon heredity (verse 13, 'not of blood'), nor upon good deeds ('the will of the flesh'), nor upon man's persuasion or choice alone ('the will of man'). For His offer of life is of grace, which means that He offers us life, not because we deserve it, but because He loves to give it (*cf.* Romans 6:23).

2 A MAN GIVES EVIDENCE
1:19–34

19 And this is the testimony of John, when the Jews sent priests and Levites from Jerusalem to ask him, 'Who are you?' ²⁰He confessed, he did not deny, but confessed, 'I am not the Christ.' ²¹And they asked him, 'What then? Are you Elijah?' He said, 'I am not.' 'Are you the prophet?' And he answered, 'No.' ²²They said to him then, 'Who are you? Let us have an answer for those who sent us. What do you say about yourself?' ²³He said, 'I am the voice of one crying in the wilderness, "Make straight the way of the Lord," as the prophet Isaiah said.'

24 Now they had been sent from the Pharisees. ²⁵They asked him, 'Then why are you baptizing, if you are neither the Christ, nor Elijah, nor the prophet?' ²⁶John answered them, 'I baptize with water; but among you stands one whom you do not know, ²⁷even he who comes after me, the thong of whose sandal I

am not worthy to untie.' ²⁸This took place in Bethany beyond the Jordan, where John was baptizing.

29 The next day he saw Jesus coming toward him, and said, 'Behold, the Lamb of God, who takes away the sin of the world! ³⁰This is he of whom I said, "After me comes a man who ranks before me, for he was before me." ³¹I myself did not know him; but for this I came baptizing with water, that he might be revealed to Israel.' ³²And John bore witness, 'I saw the Spirit descend as a dove from heaven, and it remained on him. ³³I myself did not know him; but he who sent me to baptize with water said to me, "He on whom you see the Spirit descend and remain, this is he who baptizes with the Holy Spirit." ³⁴And I have seen and have borne witness that this is the Son of God.'

If it is true that God has expressed Himself in Jesus Christ, we should expect to have important evidence from the contemporaries of Jesus as to the probability of such a claim. The first witness is a man we call John the Baptist. The Jewish historian Josephus (born AD 37) has given independent evidence of the existence of this man, and has confirmed the manner of his death described in Luke's Gospel.*

The Gospels tell us that he was the only son of an elderly couple, the priest Zacharias and his wife Elizabeth. His parents believed he was a very special gift from God and that he was a man of destiny. John grew up to be a remarkable preacher. So far as we know he was not trained at any theological college after he had left home. Since the discovery of the Dead Sea Scrolls some have suggested that he might have joined one of the religious communities, such as the Essenes, and received instruction. But his strong individualism and passionate loyalty to the Old Testament Scriptures suggests that he remained in the barren and desolate wilderness of Judea, studying the Old Testament, and preparing for his public ministry alone.

John the Baptist lived simply and ascetically, in marked contrast to many of the religious leaders of his day. He preached courageously, condemning the established order, and calling the regular 'church-goers' to forsake their wickedness and to be baptized, as a way of preparing for the coming of the Messiah (Luke 3:4-6).

* Josephus, *Antiquities of the Jews*, xviii. 5. 2.

When crowds began to flock from Jerusalem and the surrounding parts to hear John, it is not surprising that the leaders of the 'establishment' sent a small commission to find out what it was all about. It was in answer to their questions that John the Baptist tells us more about Jesus. He became convinced that Jesus was the Christ, the Messiah. He also recognized Jesus as the 'Lamb of God' and the true Son of God.

a. The Messiah (verses 19–28)

Men have always looked for a Utopia, for a new age, for a brave new world. But their hopes have always been dashed to the ground. Early in this century H. G. Wells, for example, was able to write, 'Can we doubt that presently our race will more than realise our boldest imaginations, that it will achieve unity and peace?'* By 1945 his optimistic hope that man would bring in a new age was shattered. The title of the book which expressed his disillusionment was, fittingly, *Mind at the end of its tether*.

The Jews, however, believed that God had promised a new age which would be ushered in by the coming of God's 'Anointed One', or 'Messiah', or 'Christ'. The Old Testament was full of such promises. So the Jews asked John the Baptist whether he was 'the Christ'. John's answer was clear (verses 20–23). In the East, before a king visited a province, a herald went before him to give men the opportunity to make suitable preparations. In the Baptist's view, Jesus was the Messiah, John was the herald, calling people to make ready for the coming of their king. But already the Baptist understood that this King or Messiah does not come with force but in love, for the next day he described Jesus as the 'Lamb of God'.

b. The Lamb of God (verse 29)

As the Baptist spoke perhaps he saw a flock of lambs being led to Jerusalem from the country, for the forthcoming Jewish Passover (John 2:15). The blood of the Passover lamb had once been placed on the door-posts of the homes of believing Jews when they had been slaves in Egypt. It had been a sign that saved them

* H. G. Wells, *A Short History of the World*, p. 289.

from God's judgment and from death (see Exodus 12:11–13). So when Jesus is described as the Lamb of God, it implies that He would shed His blood to save men from judgment and death.

Certainly John had been thinking about the words of the prophet Isaiah (verse 23). From Isaiah John would know that the Messiah could deliver God's people only through suffering. The 'suffering servant' of Isaiah's prophecies would be led 'as a lamb to the slaughter' and would be 'wounded for our transgressions and bruised for our iniquities'. In a remarkable way these words were going to be fulfilled in the death of Jesus Christ, who would die 'to take away the sin of the world'. In the Bible sin means 'missing the mark' or 'breaking the law'. It is because we are all sinners by God's standards that someone is needed to come and 'bear away sin'. But who can forgive sins but One who comes from God and identifies Himself with men? The Baptist believed that Jesus did just that, when he called Him both 'Lamb of God' and 'Son of God'.

c. The Son of God (verses 30–34)

The brothers of Jesus were cousins of John the Baptist. So probably John and Jesus had met before. But the Baptist tells us that he was not certain that Jesus was the Messiah until a remarkable event took place. Jesus asked to be baptized by John. Although John did not feel worthy to baptize Jesus, he realized that God had a purpose in it. God gave him a sign that day that Jesus was not only the Messiah, but in a unique sense *God's Son* (verse 34). There is no suggestion here that Jesus had sinned, but the significance of Jesus's baptism seems to be that He was identifying Himself with sinners.

This Gospel argues that Jesus is uniquely and eternally the Son of God, or God become man. We shall need to look carefully at the reasons for such a staggering claim. But Christians believe that, because Jesus is both God and man, He is able in a unique way to bring God and man together.

3 FOUR MORE WITNESSES
1:35–51

35 The next day again John was standing with two of his disciples; ³⁶and he looked at Jesus as he walked, and said, 'Behold, the Lamb of God!' ³⁷The two disciples heard him say this, and they followed Jesus. ³⁸Jesus turned, and saw them following, and said to them, 'What do you seek?' And they said to him, 'Rabbi' (which means Teacher), 'where are you staying?' ³⁹He said to them, 'Come and see.' They came and saw where he was staying; and they stayed with him that day, for it was about the tenth hour. ⁴⁰One of the two who heard John speak, and followed him, was Andrew, Simon Peter's brother. ⁴¹He first found his brother Simon, and said to him, 'We have found the Messiah' (which means Christ). ⁴²He brought him to Jesus. Jesus looked at him, and said, 'So you are Simon the son of John? You shall be called Cephas' (which means Rock).

43 The next day Jesus decided to go to Galilee. And he found Philip and said to him, 'Follow me.' ⁴⁴Now Philip was from Bethsaida, the city of Andrew and Peter. ⁴⁵Philip found Nathanael, and said to him, 'We have found him of whom Moses in the law and also the prophets wrote, Jesus of Nazareth, the son of Joseph.' ⁴⁶Nathanael said to him, 'Can anything good come out of Nazareth?' Philip said to him, 'Come and see.' ⁴⁷Jesus saw Nathanael coming to him, and said of him, 'Behold, an Israelite indeed, in whom is no guile!' ⁴⁸Nathanael said to him, 'How do you know me?' Jesus answered him, 'Before Philip called you, when you were under the fig tree, I saw you.' ⁴⁹Nathanael answered him, 'Rabbi, you are the Son of God! You are the King of Israel!' ⁵⁰Jesus answered him, 'Because I said to you, I saw you under the fig tree, do you believe? You shall see greater things than these.' ⁵¹And he said to him, 'Truly, truly, I say to you, you will see heaven opened, and the angels of God ascending and descending upon the Son of man.'

Some people might discount the evidence of John the Baptist as prejudiced. He was related to the family of Jesus. He was a preacher, a professional. He had a special relationship to Jesus as a 'forerunner', a 'herald'. The next four witnesses are all totally different from one another and from John the Baptist. They are not 'sons of the manse' or of the Temple. They are working men, tough fishermen. They are practical men of affairs and not starry-eyed idealists.

Andrew, for example, was a fisherman who had been attracted by the preaching of John the Baptist. He was a humble man who was prepared to play second fiddle to his more extrovert brother, Simon. But quiet and unassuming as he may well have been, *he was prepared to spend time in discovering who Jesus really was* (verses 38–40). Furthermore, once he was sure that Jesus was the Messiah, he could not keep the discovery to himself (verse 41).

Simon (verses 41, 42), a real extrovert, was as enthusiastic as he was impulsive, as unreliable as he was on occasions brave. He was as likely to swear violently as to make lofty resolutions passionately. But Jesus realized his potential and recognized that he would one day be a great leader in the church. He would one day live up to his new name, Peter (a rock). The way in which this man's character was moulded is part of the evidence to the unique personality of Jesus, and His influence on men.

Philip (verses 43, 44), who came from the same town as Peter and Andrew, was slow and unimpressive. He often lacked faith and vision (John 6:5–7). He was slow to understand spiritual truth (John 14:8–11) and to take initiative (John 12:20–22). But there is a certain down-to-earth, practical side to his character which makes him an important witness. It is encouraging to notice that Jesus does not overlook 'slow and ordinary' people. On the contrary Jesus went to Galilee to find him, and to invite him to become one of His disciples (verse 43).

Nathanael (verses 45–51) was an intellectual. It was a Jewish custom to sit and meditate upon the Scriptures under the shady branches of the fig tree (verse 48). This is what Nathanael loved to do. Because of his knowledge he was at first sceptical of the claim that Jesus was the Messiah (verse 46). His scepticism was not without reason, for Nazareth had already produced a number of fanatics who had falsely called themselves Messiah. But neither was it without prejudice; *and prejudice often hinders a man from discovering the truth*. When Nathanael meets Jesus, however, his prejudices are dispelled. How was this possible? (i) His search for the truth was 'without guile' (verse 47). He was transparently sincere and open to truth. (ii) He was prepared to make the effort to look at the evidence. He was willing to 'come and see' (verse 46). (iii) He was impressed by Jesus' superhuman knowledge (verses 48, 49). (iv) He was prepared to acknowledge Jesus as God's Son and Messiah. When we are prepared to go as far as this man in our search, we shall not be far from discovering the truth.

Jesus then promised Nathanael further knowledge about Himself (verses 50–52). Perhaps Nathanael had been reading from the book of Genesis the story of Jacob's dream (see Genesis 28:10–17). Jacob was running away from home after tricking and deceiving his father Isaac and his brother Esau. In his dream he saw a ladder stretching from heaven to earth with angels climbing up and down it. This was a sign to him that God was with him. Jesus takes up this theme and tells Nathanael that he will come to recognize that Jesus has come to bring heaven to earth, God to man, man to God. God still reveals this truth to those who seek Him sincerely and with all their heart.

4 THE FIRST SIGN
2:1–11

1 On the third day there was a marriage at Cana in Galilee, and the mother of Jesus was there; ²Jesus also was invited to the marriage, with his disciples. ³When the wine failed, the mother of Jesus said to him, 'They have no wine.' ⁴And Jesus said to her, 'O woman, what have you to do with me? My hour has not yet come.' ⁵His mother said to the servants, 'Do whatever he tells you.' ⁶Now six stone jars were standing there, for the Jewish rites of purification, each holding twenty or thirty gallons. ⁷Jesus said to them, 'Fill the jars with water.' And they filled them up to the brim. ⁸He said to them, 'Now draw some out, and take it to the steward of the feast.' So they took it. ⁹When the steward of the feast tasted the water now become

wine, and did not know where it came from (though the servants who had drawn the water knew), the steward of the feast called the bridegroom [10]and said to him, 'Every man serves the good wine first; and when men have drunk freely, then the poor wine; but you have kept the good wine until now.' [11]This, the first of his signs, Jesus did at Cana in Galilee, and manifested his glory; and his disciples believed in him.

The writer now describes an incident that would be regarded as a scoop by every Fleet Street reporter. It is a story packed with human interest. A wedding. A crisis in the catering arrangements at the reception. The miraculous turning of water into wine. A happy ending.

It took place in the village of Cana, a few miles north-east of Nazareth. Cana was probably on the site of the modern village of Kefr Kenna, on the dusty road to the Lake of Galilee. We can perhaps imagine its terraced houses with their flat roofs, and the gardens and orchards which, it is said, produced some of the best pomegranates in Palestine. It is possible that Nathanael lived here, and that Jesus and His disciples stayed with him before going on to the wedding. Mary, the mother of Jesus, seems to have been an important guest (verses 1, 3).

In Jewish law the wedding of a virgin took place on a Wednesday, and the wedding ceremony itself was held late in the evening after a feast. The festivities then continued for several days, and this of course increased the sense of social disaster that the couple and their parents would have felt when they ran out of wine (verse 3).

The story of the way in which Jesus turned water into wine raises two important questions in our search for truth.

a. Is it reasonable to believe in such a miracle?

Before we dismiss the miraculous as 'unscientific', we would do well to consider three propositions which here can be stated only briefly.

1. *My estimate of miracles will depend on my estimate of Jesus Christ.* If Jesus is no more than a great prophet or teacher, then I would do well to examine His miraculous claims critically. But if, on other grounds, I am persuaded that He is God become man, then

I shall not be surprised at the evidence of divine and supernatural power. It would not then be incredible that the God who provides both wine and water should turn the water into wine.

2. *My estimate of miracles must take into account the historical documents of the New Testament.* There is as good documentary evidence for the miracles of Jesus as for His teaching. If we accept the one we must have good reasons for rejecting the other. In this story there are several authentic eyewitness touches which make it very difficult to dismiss the story as make-believe. For example, it was appropriate that the *bridegroom* is addressed by the steward (verse 9). According to Jewish custom the bridegroom paid the bills! It is interesting also that the 'best man' or friend of the bridegroom is not mentioned. The Talmud tells us that in Galilee (but not in Judea: see John 3:29) 'friends of the bridegroom' were not employed. Again, the words of Jesus to His mother, 'O woman, what have you to do with me? My hour has not yet come' are hardly the words we would expect to find in a fabricated, make-believe story. They are, of course, not as harsh as they sound. 'Woman' (Greek *gunai*) is a word of respect. Jesus addresses His mother in the same way when He is dying on the cross (John 19:26). 'What have you to do with me?' is an idiomatic expression and probably means 'My way is not your way'. 'My hour has not yet come' (verse 4) probably means 'My time is not your time'.*

3. *My estimate of miracles must take into account their meaning and purpose.* It is the meaninglessness of some of the miracles in the apocryphal Gospels which make them incredible. But John rightly calls the miracles of Jesus 'signs'. Jesus is not a magician but a teacher, and the miracles authenticate His message, reveal His character and the purpose of His coming, and are significant visual aids. If we try to 'explain away' the miracles of Jesus, we shall distrust His teaching. This leads us to the second question.

b. What is the purpose of this miracle?

John's explanation lies in the phrase 'Jesus . . . manifested his glory; and his disciples believed in him' (verse 11). In other words Jesus

* For further reading: C. S. Lewis, *Miracles* and F. F. Bruce, *The New Testament Documents*.

let the disciples know a little more about Himself and about what He had come to do, when He turned the water into wine at that wedding reception at Cana. He showed how He cares about the joyful occasions of life as well as the sad. He showed His concern for domestic as well as ecclesiastical problems. He showed that there is nothing He cannot do in His own time and in His own way, if people will trust Him (like Mary, verse 3) and obey Him (like the servants, verses 5, 7 and 8).

For the Jews a wedding was very much a religious ceremony, and they would remember that the New Age which the Messiah would introduce was sometimes likened to a joyful wedding-feast. Jesus had come to introduce a New Age better than the old, even as the new wine was the best at that wedding. As the disciples saw this evidence of His love and power, and this sign that He had every right to be called Messiah, they began to put their faith in Him (verse 11).

5 A VISIT TO JERUSALEM
2:12–25

12 After this he went down to Capernaum, with his mother and his brothers and his disciples; and there they stayed for a few days.

13 The Passover of the Jews was at hand, and Jesus went up to Jerusalem. 14In the temple he found those who were selling oxen and sheep and pigeons, and the money-changers at their business. 15And making a whip of cords, he drove them all, with the sheep and oxen, out of the temple; and he poured out the coins of the money-changers and overturned their tables. 16And he told those who sold the pigeons, 'Take these things away; you shall not make my Father's house a house of trade.' 17His disciples remembered that it was written, 'Zeal for thy house will consume me.' 18The Jews then said to him, 'What sign have you to show us for doing this?' 19Jesus

answered them, 'Destroy this temple, and in three days I will raise it up.' ²⁰The Jews then said, 'It has taken forty-six years to build this temple, and will you raise it up in three days?' ²¹But he spoke of the temple of his body. ²²When therefore he was raised from the dead, his disciples remembered that he had said this; and they believed the scripture and the word which Jesus had spoken.

23 Now when he was in Jerusalem at the Passover feast, many believed in his name when they saw the signs which he did; ²⁴but Jesus did not trust himself to them, ²⁵because he knew all men and needed no one to bear witness of man; for he himself knew what was in man.

When Jesus visited Jerusalem it soon became clear that His teaching would not be welcomed by the religious leaders. Jerusalem was always busy, especially at Passover time, which, by our reckoning, would be some time in the middle of April. Crowds thronged the streets; sometimes as many as two and a half million Jews assembled in Jerusalem during the Passover. Travellers bargained in the markets. Sightseers idly gaped at Herod's magnificent Temple.

It was, however, within the Temple precincts that Jesus saw so much to disturb Him. John alone records a 'cleansing of the Temple' at the beginning of Jesus' ministry. But it is clear that His purpose in selecting this incident is to show us Jesus as the Messiah at the very start of His public ministry acting not only in love but in righteousness. Jesus saw that the institutional religion of His day was riddled with many evils.

a. Dishonesty (verses 14–17)

The money-changers (verse 14) changed ordinary money into Temple currency in order that the pilgrims could pay the Temple tax. It has been estimated that the annual revenue from the Temple tax was about £75,000 (or roughly $180,000) and that the money-changers made an annual *profit* of £9,000 (or $22,000)!

It is also likely that those who sold oxen, sheep and pigeons charged exorbitant prices. It has been estimated that a pair of doves could cost as little as ninepence outside the Temple, and as much as fifteen shillings inside. Nevertheless, the worshippers would have to pay the higher price because it was very likely that animals bought outside the Temple precincts would be rejected as unsuitable for worship by the Temple inspectors!

Jesus is passionately concerned about social justice. His action (verses 15, 16) reveals His anger against evil, as well as His love for those who were being exploited.

b. Hypocrisy

It is certain that many who worshipped in the Temple were forgetting the true end of worship in using the complicated sacrificial system of the Jews. In the same way, formal religious observance in the church today often has precisely the same effect. 'Take these things away' suggests that Jesus had come to abolish the Jewish system of worship altogether, and to make possible a direct and spiritual worship of God without elaborate ritual and ceremony. The disciples realized that such zeal for pure and spiritual worship would lead to His death (verse 17). Indeed they understood later that His death and resurrection would be the means of establishing such worship (verses 19–22).

c. Prejudice (verses 18–21)

Men do not like their traditional forms of worship criticized, nor their selfishness and greed shown up. The question 'What sign have you to show us for doing this?' (verse 18) was the first sign of hostility to the claims and actions of Jesus. Jesus' enigmatic answer, which was later used against Him at His trial (Mark 14:58; Matthew 26:61; 27:40), was deliberately obscure, probably because of the prejudice and lack of humility of the questioners. Even the sign of the resurrection failed to convince those who would not humbly seek to know the truth. The disciples realized later, however, that the death and resurrection of Jesus fulfilled the promises of the Old Testament as well as the words of Jesus Himself (verse 22).

d. Superficiality (verses 23–25)

Even those who were not hostile to Jesus were superficial in their belief. They were ready to follow a worker of 'miracles', but not

33

always a worker of righteousness. The love of Jesus was attractive. The righteousness of Jesus was demanding. It was easier to accept comfort than to face demands. Jesus knew the difference between sincere and superficial belief, for He knew men's inmost thoughts (verse 25). He knew that true belief would arise out of a genuine need for forgiveness, as well as a conviction that Christ alone, and not animal sacrifices, could provide it. True belief would involve forsaking sin—dishonesty, hypocrisy, hostility to Jesus, superficiality and the rest—as well as following Jesus. The new life could not be received unless the old life was renounced. Jesus knew all this. So He would not commit Himself to men, unless they were ready to commit themselves fully to Him (verse 24). We cannot follow Jesus without forsaking sin.

6 JESUS MEETS A SINCERE CHURCHMAN
3:1–21

1 Now there was a man of the Pharisees, named Nicodemus, a ruler of the Jews. ²This man came to Jesus by night and said to him, 'Rabbi, we know that you are a teacher come from God; for no one can do these signs that you do, unless God is with him.' ³Jesus answered him, 'Truly, truly, I say to you, unless one is born anew, he cannot see the kingdom of God.' ⁴Nicodemus said to him, 'How can a man be born when he is old? Can he enter a second time into his mother's womb and be born?' ⁵Jesus answered, 'Truly, truly, I say to you, unless one is born of water and the Spirit, he cannot enter the kingdom of God. ⁶That which is born of the flesh is flesh, and that which is born of the Spirit is spirit. ⁷Do not marvel that I said to you, "You must be born anew." ⁸The wind blows where it wills, and you hear the sound of it, but you do not know whence it comes or whither it goes; so it is with every one who is born of the Spirit.' ⁹Nicodemus said to him, 'How can this be?' ¹⁰Jesus answered him, 'Are you a teacher of Israel, and yet you do not understand this? ¹¹Truly, truly, I say to you, we speak

of what we know, and bear witness to what we have seen; but you do not receive our testimony. ¹²If I have told you earthly things and you do not believe, how can you believe if I tell you heavenly things? ¹³No one has ascended into heaven but he who descended from heaven, the Son of man. ¹⁴And as Moses lifted up the serpent in the wilderness, so must the Son of man be lifted up, ¹⁵that whoever believes in him may have eternal life.'

16 For God so loved the world that he gave his only Son, that whoever believes in him should not perish but have eternal life. ¹⁷For God sent the Son into the world, not to condemn the world, but that the world might be saved through him. ¹⁸He who believes in him is not condemned; he who does not believe is condemned already, because he has not believed in the name of the only Son of God. ¹⁹And this is the judgment, that the light has come into the world, and men loved darkness rather than light, because their deeds were evil. ²⁰For every one who does evil hates the light, and does not come to the light, lest his deeds should be exposed. ²¹But he who does what is true comes to the light, that it may be clearly seen that his deeds have been wrought in God.

Some years ago a nurse wrote these words in a letter: 'For several years now, although I've gone to church, read my Bible and really tried to be a true Christian, *I've always felt there was something missing . . .*' It was only later that she found a personal faith. The late Bishop Handley Moule described his religious life as an undergraduate: 'I was aware, as time went on, that my contact with the Lord, whom I saw known and loved before my eyes, was only (if I may put it so) *at second hand.*'* From these examples we see that it is possible to be religious and not Christian, to know about God and not to know Him in a first-hand, personal way.

Nicodemus was a religious man like that. As a Pharisee he would have prayed and read the Scriptures and attended a place of worship regularly. He was moreover something of an expert in religion, '*the* teacher of Israel',† and a distinguished member of the Jewish Sanhedrin. It is likely that he was a man of upright character, generosity (giving tithes to the poor) and humility (notice how he addresses Jesus in verse 2). But he needed to know how to enter the kingdom of God, and how to enjoy God's rule and God's life

---

* Harford and MacDonald, *Bishop Handley Moule*, p. 49.
† The definite article is used in the Greek of verse 10.

personally. He came 'by night' (verse 2) possibly because he preferred that men should not notice his interest in Jesus. It would not
be easy for a man in his position to be too closely associated with
Jesus of Nazareth. Possibly too he wanted an unhurried time to ask
all his questions. In speaking to Nicodemus, Jesus emphasized
three truths.

a. The necessity for the new birth (verses 3–8)

Personal knowledge of God is possible only through spiritual re-
birth. A man cannot enjoy physical life unless he is born, and neither
can he enjoy spiritual life unless he is born anew (see verse 6). This
involves receiving a new life rather than turning over a new leaf.
For man cannot save himself. He is spiritually 'dead' until God
gives him life. Without the new birth a man can no more appreciate
spiritual truths than a dead man can appreciate life or a blind man
appreciate the beauties of the sunset (see verses 3, 5).

Nicodemus (verse 4) could not understand such revolutionary
teaching, although the Old Testament had spoken of it (see
Ezekiel 36:25–27). Like most of us he found it easier to understand material rather than spiritual concepts. Jesus reminds him
that it is more important to experience the 'new birth' than to
understand it (verses 7, 8). We may not understand how the wind
'works', but we can see its effects as it moves the leaves in the
trees. We may not understand the working of God's Spirit in our
lives, but once we have experienced this, we shall be able to say 'we
speak of what we know' (verse 11). So the new birth is the only
way into God's family. It is the gateway to the enjoyment of God's
kingdom.

b. The necessity for Christ's death (verses 14, 15)

Nicodemus was still puzzled. How could he experience the new
birth (verse 9)? Jesus first asserts His authority for speaking with
such certainty (verses 11–13). Then He gives Nicodemus an Old
Testament illustration (verse 14). It is true that man deserves death,
not life. The Israelites had learnt this in the well-known story in
Numbers 21:5–9. Because of their grumbling and rebellion against

36

God, God had allowed a plague of poisonous snakes to bring death to many of them as a judgment upon their sin. But when they cried out to God to save them, He ordered Moses to make a serpent of brass and to lift it up on a pole, and God promised that those who looked upon the serpent, and believed His promise, would live.

The lesson is clear. There can be no 'life' without death. Man could not be saved from God's judgment unless Christ was lifted up (like the serpent) and bore the judgment man deserved. That is what Jesus came to do, for, as John comments, 'God so loved the world that he *gave* his only begotten Son . . .' (verse 16).

c. The necessity for man's response (verses 16–21)

It was only those who believed God's promise, and who looked to the serpent, who lived. So it is only those who believe God's promise and who look to the Lord Jesus Christ as the Son of God (verse 18) and as the One who saves us from the consequences of sin (verse 17) who receive eternal life (verses 15, 16 and 18).

But what happens if I do not believe in Jesus Christ in this way? John tells us that Jesus came into the world primarily to save men, not to judge them (verse 17). But the shining of the sun inevitably brings shadows. To turn our back on the sun is to deepen the shadows. To refuse life is to choose death. To reject salvation is to invite condemnation. An honest seeker (verse 21) will not cover up his failure and sins. He will come to the light and find life. But another, who loves darkness rather than light, will prefer to cover up his sins, and so will be self-condemned (verses 18–20). This is the judgment. It happens every time a man turns his back upon Jesus Christ.

22 After this Jesus and his disciples went into the land of Judea; there he remained with them and baptized. ²³John also was baptizing at Aenon near Salim, because there was much water there; and people came and were baptized. ²⁴For John had not yet been put in prison.

25 Now a discussion arose between John's disciples and a Jew over purifying. ²⁶And they came to John, and said to him, 'Rabbi, he who was with you beyond the Jordan, to whom you bore witness, here he is, baptizing, and all are going to him.' ²⁷John answered, 'No one can receive anything except what is given him from heaven. ²⁸You yourselves bear me witness, that I said, I am not the Christ, but I have been sent before him. ²⁹He who has the bride is the bridegroom; the friend of the bridegroom, who stands and hears him, rejoices greatly at the bridegroom's voice; therefore this joy of mine is now full. ³⁰He must increase, but I must decrease.'

31 He who comes from above is above all; he who is of the earth belongs to the earth, and of the earth he speaks; he who comes from heaven is above all. ³²He bears witness to what he has seen and heard, yet no one receives his testimony; ³³he who receives his testimony sets his seal to this, that God is true. ³⁴For he whom God has sent utters the words of God, for it is not by measure that he gives the Spirit; ³⁵the Father loves the Son, and has given all things into his hand. ³⁶He who believes in the Son has eternal life; he who does not obey the Son shall not see life, but the wrath of God rests upon him.

How seriously must we take the teaching of Jesus? His words on the necessity for the new birth and the certainty of judgment are serious enough. But are they not the sincere belief of one great prophet amongst others? Is Jesus more than a prophet? Is He unique?

Some of the disciples of John the Baptist were loth to believe that Jesus was greater than their leader. They were sad when they saw that John was taking second place to Jesus. Many more people were going to Jesus to be baptized than to John the Baptist (verses 22–26). We have further evidence here from the Baptist himself.

a. More evidence from John the Baptist (verses 25–30)

John once again makes it clear that it is Jesus who is the Messiah (verses 26, 27). He describes his relationship to Jesus as that of a 'best man' to a bridegroom (verse 29). At an eastern wedding 'the friend of the bridegroom' went ahead of the bride and groom to make all necessary preparations for the wedding festivities. He even guarded the bridal chamber, and would open the door only when he heard and recognized the bridegroom's voice, and could bring the happy couple together. Then he would be glad that his job was done, and that he could fade more and more into the background. So John the Baptist rejoiced that men and women were increasingly coming not to him but to Jesus. It would be absurd for the best man to be jealous of the bridegroom! John's task was to fade into the background. He rightly says, 'He must increase, but I must decrease.'

b. The evidence of John the Evangelist (verses 31–36)

These verses are almost certainly the comment of the Evangelist rather than of John the Baptist. They record John's conviction that Jesus is not only the Messiah, but the Son of God (verse 35). It is because Jesus is in this unique relationship to God that His words are authoritative and true and tremendously important. If we wanted to know all about the Royal Family, our best authority would be someone from that family. If we want to know about God, we need to hear someone from God. It is because Jesus is 'from above' that He is above all other teachers (verse 31). It is because He is 'from heaven' (verse 31) that He can tell us from personal experience about the life of heaven, and the truths of God. It is because God has sent Jesus filled with the Spirit, in a unique sense, that the words of Jesus are the very words of God. For all that we need to know about God and His life has been given to Jesus to reveal to us (verses 34 and 35).

If the words of Jesus are the very words of God (John is sure of this, verse 33; others reject it, verse 32), then they must be taken with extreme seriousness. They become matters of life and death. The issue is this: If a man believes on Christ he receives eternal life. On the other hand to disobey the words of Christ means to disobey God Himself, and to face here and now His displeasure (verse 36).

c. The wrath of God (verse 36)

There is one problem in this passage which all must face honestly. Can we believe that the wrath of God is compatible with the love of God? John, the apostle of love, apparently sees no difficulty. But some modern thinkers are appalled by such a doctrine.

When we speak of God's wrath we are of course using a human term to describe a characteristic of God. It is hard for us to understand how a man can be angry and exercise wrath without vindictiveness and even hatred entering in. This is not so with God. Wrath is the reverse side of His love. It is a way of describing a loving God's hatred of sin and evil and disobedience and all that spoils the lives of those whom He loves. As the light of the sun destroys germs, and the light switched on in a room banishes darkness, so God's sinless and perfect presence banishes sin, and His wrath rests upon the sinner. Jesus has already shown His wrath in taking action against the sin and hypocrisy in the Temple at Jerusalem (see chapter 2). The wrath of God teaches us that God does not stand by and condone sin and injustice and evil in the world. He takes action against it. It shows us that there is nothing sentimental about the love of God. It reminds us that we cannot 'get away with' sin.

We have already learnt from the story of the brass serpent that Christ bore God's judgment upon sin when He died on the cross. Jesus had never sinned, but He died in the place of sinners. He was perfectly obedient, but He bore the guilt of the disobedient. That is why it is possible for those who believe on Jesus Christ to be delivered from the wrath of God, and to receive eternal life.

8 JESUS SPEAKS TO A WOMAN OF THE WORLD

4:1–30

1 Now when the Lord knew that the Pharisees had heard that Jesus was making and baptizing more disciples than John ²(although Jesus himself did not baptize, but only his disciples), ³he left Judea and departed again to Galilee. ⁴He had to pass through Samaria. ⁵So he came to a city of Samaria, called Sychar, near the field that Jacob gave to his son Joseph. ⁶Jacob's well was there, and so Jesus, wearied as he was with his journey, sat down beside the well. It was about the sixth hour.

7 There came a woman of Samaria to draw water. Jesus said to her, 'Give me a drink.' ⁸For his disciples had gone away into the city to buy food. ⁹The Samaritan woman said to him, 'How is it that you, a Jew, ask a drink of me, a woman of Samaria?' For Jews have no dealings with Samaritans. ¹⁰Jesus answered her, 'If you knew the gift of God, and who it is that is saying to you, "Give me a drink," you would have asked him, and he would have given you living water.' ¹¹The woman said to him, 'Sir, you have nothing to draw with, and the well is deep; where do you get that living water? ¹²Are you greater than our father Jacob, who gave us the well, and drank from it himself, and his sons, and his cattle?' ¹³Jesus said to her, 'Every one who drinks of this water will thirst again, ¹⁴but whoever drinks of the water that I shall give him will never thirst; the water that I shall give him will become in him a spring of water welling up to eternal life.' ¹⁵The woman said to him, 'Sir, give me this water, that I may not thirst, nor come here to draw.'

16 Jesus said to her, 'Go, call your husband, and come here.' ¹⁷The woman answered him, 'I have no husband.' Jesus said to her, 'You are right in saying, "I have no husband"; ¹⁸for you have had five husbands, and he whom you now have is not your husband; this you said truly.' ¹⁹The woman said to him, 'Sir, I perceive that you are a prophet. ²⁰Our fathers worshipped on this mountain; and you say that in Jerusalem is the place where men ought to worship.' ²¹Jesus said to her, 'Woman, believe me, the hour is coming when neither on this mountain

nor in Jerusalem will you worship the Father. [22]You worship what you do not know; we worship what we know, for salvation is from the Jews. [23]But the hour is coming, and now is, when the true worshippers will worship the Father in spirit and truth, for such the Father seeks to worship him. [24]God is spirit, and those who worship him must worship in spirit and truth.' [25]The woman said to him, 'I know that Messiah is coming (he who is called Christ); when he comes, he will show us all things.' [26]Jesus said to her, 'I who speak to you am he.'

27 Just then his disciples came. They marvelled that he was talking with a woman, but none said, 'What do you wish?' or, 'Why are you talking with her?' [28]So the woman left her water jar, and went away into the city, and said to the people, [29]'Come, see a man who told me all that I ever did. Can this be the Christ?' [30]They went out of the city and were coming to him.

The problem of race relations is not a modern one. When Jesus left Judea and decided to take the short cut to Galilee through Samaria, he entered a country which was still very sensitive about its relationship with the rest of Palestine. The problem began as far back as 720 BC, when the Assyrians conquered the northern kingdom of Samaria, and encouraged widespread immigration from Babylon and other countries (see 2 Kings 17:24). There followed the inevitable intermarrying between Samaritan Jews and immigrants. In the eyes of the orthodox Jew, it was a terrible crime to lose racial purity, and from that time on the Jews and Samaritans hated and despised one another (verse 9). As we know from this story the separation was so deep that the Samaritans had even built their own temple for worship on Mount Gerizim (see verse 21).

It was at the hottest time of day (12 o'clock—for the Jewish day runs from 6 a.m. to 6 p.m.) that Jesus sat down, tired, thirsty and hot, at the well of Sychar (verses 5, 6). This well can almost certainly be identified today.

When Jesus first meets the woman from Samaria she is a sharp-tongued, hard and rather cynical woman of the world, who seemed glad to score a few cheap points off an interesting man. By the end of her conversation with Jesus she is so impressed that she forgets why she ever came to the well, leaves her water-pot behind and rushes home to tell her associates all about Him (verses 28, 29).

If we contrast this story with the interview with Nicodemus

(chapter 3), we see that Jesus is concerned about the Samaritan as well as the Jew. He seeks the ignorant as well as the learned. He will talk with the poor as well as the rich. He cares for women as well as men—and remember that the Jews had a prayer which stated 'Blessed art Thou O Lord . . . who hast not made me a woman'! He loved the morally corrupt as well as the morally upright. His love is for all men. His 'life' is offered to all. He came, as the Samaritans said later (4:42), to be 'the Saviour of the world'. Jesus indeed recognized no social, racial or religious barriers which He could not overcome. There are no second-class citizens in His kingdom. An orthodox Jew, who became a Christian, was able to write a few years later: 'There is neither Jew nor Greek, there is neither slave nor free, there is neither male nor female; for you are all one in Christ Jesus' (see Paul's letter to the Galatians 3:28).

The Rabbis had a saying, 'A man should not salute a woman in a public place, not even his own wife.' No wonder the woman was surprised that Jesus spoke to her—a woman, and a Samaritan (verse 9). We can perhaps imagine her, hands on her hips and a coy look on her face. Jesus, however, was quite prepared to flout convention for the sake of a needy person. As He talks to her we can see that He taught her what her deepest needs were.

a. Spiritual rather than physical (verses 7–15)

At first, when Jesus spoke about 'living water', she thought perhaps of fresh running water from a stream instead of from a well (verse 11). Or maybe she is simply being flippant. Certainly she did not believe that Jesus could improve on Jacob's method of drawing water (notice her sly dig that Jacob was as much the 'father' of the Samaritans as the Jews—verse 12). When Jesus talks about spiritual needs (verses 13, 14), she appears deliberately dumb, and says in effect, 'If you can save me trouble, then give me this water' (verse 15). But spiritual needs are more important than physical ones. We all have physical needs, but we also have an underlying spiritual thirst that can be satisfied only by Jesus Christ. Water satisfies physical thirst temporarily. The life that Jesus offers to man is permanently satisfying and wells up within man's inmost being like a bubbling spring (verse 14). No doubt this woman

43

thought that sex experience would bring her satisfaction. Jesus taught her that her need was spiritual more than physical.

b. Moral rather than intellectual (verses 16–26)

With a sure touch Jesus puts His finger on her real problem in order to help her to face up to it. 'Go, call your husband, and come here' (verse 16). None of us likes to face up to moral failure in our lives. This woman was no exception and in a short time she was trying to evade the real moral issue with an intellectual red-herring on a matter of controversy between the Jews and Samaritans (verses 19, 20)—a quick move on her part to get out of an awkward situation. Jesus' answer introduces a further truth. What really matters is not *where* a man worships but *how* he worships. 'God is spirit', therefore He is not confined to a particular place, or to a particular form or material expression of worship. The time has now come when it is possible to worship God 'in the Spirit' and 'from the heart'. We can now worship God 'in truth', because the only true way to God has been revealed (verses 23, 24). In a word, our *moral* and spiritual problems are not dealt with by deciding which church to belong to or by tightening up on our religious duties, or by solving all our controversial, intellectual problems. They can be solved only by the new life in the spirit which is possible through Jesus Christ.

The woman does not yet fully understand, but Jesus shows Himself to her (verse 25) as the Messiah who reveals God in truth and makes possible worship 'by the Spirit'. The mention of the water-pot (verse 28) is surely the mark of an eyewitness account.

9 THE PRIORITIES OF JESUS
4:31-54

31 Meanwhile the disciples besought him, saying, 'Rabbi, eat.'
[32]But he said to them, 'I have food to eat of which you do not
know.' [33]So the disciples said to one another, 'Has any one
brought him food?' [34]Jesus said to them, 'My food is to do the
will of him who sent me, and to accomplish his work. [35]Do you
not say, "There are yet four months, then comes the harvest"?
I tell you, lift up your eyes, and see how the fields are already
white for harvest. [36]He who reaps receives wages, and gathers
fruit for eternal life, so that sower and reaper may rejoice together. [37]For here the saying holds true, "One sows and another
reaps." [38]I sent you to reap that for which you did not labour;
others have laboured, and you have entered into their labour.'

39 Many Samaritans from that city believed in him because
of the woman's testimony, 'He told me all that I ever did.'
[40]So when the Samaritans came to him, they asked him to stay
with them; and he stayed there two days. [41]And many more
believed because of his word. [42]They said to the woman, 'It is
no longer because of your words that we believe, for we have
heard for ourselves, and we know that this is indeed the Saviour
of the world.'

43 After the two days he departed to Galilee. [44]For Jesus
himself testified that a prophet has no honour in his own
country. [45]So when he came to Galilee, the Galileans welcomed
him, having seen all that he had done in Jerusalem at the
feast, for they too had gone to the feast.

46 So he came again to Cana in Galilee, where he had made
the water wine. And at Capernaum there was an official whose
son was ill. [47]When he heard that Jesus had come from Judea
to Galilee, he went and begged him to come down and heal his
son, for he was at the point of death. [48]Jesus therefore said to
him, 'Unless you see signs and wonders you will not believe.'
[49]The official said to him, 'Sir, come down before my child
dies.' [50]Jesus said to him, 'Go; your son will live.' The man
believed the word that Jesus spoke to him and went his way.
[51]As he was going down, his servants met him and told him
that his son was living. [52]So he asked them the hour when he
began to mend, and they said to him, 'Yesterday at the seventh

hour the fever left him.' ⁵³The father knew that was the hour when Jesus had said to him, 'Your son will live'; and he himself believed, and all his household. ⁵⁴This was now the second sign that Jesus did when he had come from Judea to Galilee.

Jesus' emphasis upon the spiritual needs of the woman of Samaria leads to a discussion with His disciples about His own purpose in coming into the world and His own priorities. His description of His mission in the world, and that of His disciples, is very different from the popular view that many people hold. Some people believe that Christianity needs to be reinterpreted entirely in secular terms. Unless the church is feeding the hungry, establishing social justice, housing the homeless, speaking out against war, she has totally failed, we are told. Jesus Himself cared both for the bodies and the souls of men, for their physical as well as spiritual needs, for their temporal as well as eternal concerns. He cared for the whole man; and so of course should the Christian church. But Jesus did not 'secularize' religion. He had clear priorities. For Him the spiritual was more important than the physical, the eternal than the temporal. In this passage He emphasizes three things about His mission in the world.

a. The importance of obedience (verses 31–34)

The disciples of Jesus are anxious about His physical needs. They know He must be hungry (verse 31). Bound as they are by routine and convention, they no doubt wonder why He spends His time talking to such a woman, when He could be taking refreshment. Jesus' answer shows that it is doing God's will and completing what His Father wants Him to do which alone satisfies the inner man (verse 34). It is not only gourmets who are apt to forget that truth. It is through obedience that Jesus fulfils His mission to the world—an obedience which led Him to death on the Roman gallows. It is through obedience that we may share in His mission to the world, and discover inner satisfaction.

b. The importance of vision (verses 35–38)

The world is like a field full of crops ready to be reaped. The farmer may say there is four months until harvest. Jesus can say to the disciples that even *now* there are many people ready to be gathered into His kingdom. The disciples seemed blind both to the needs of those around them (such as the Samaritan woman) and to the opportunities of working with Jesus to meet those needs. In an age which can bring the sufferings of the world into our homes through television, many of us seem to be as blind as the disciples in failing to see and to meet man's physical and spiritual problems. However, Jesus promises that if we work with Him the rewards and the results of such service will be lasting and joyful. The Christian is not called to 'do good' in the world for his own glory, and for the pleasure it gives him; but rather to work together with others, in obedience to Christ's command and for eternal ends (verses 37, 38). Only Jesus Christ can give a man this view of service to the community.

c. The importance of faith (verses 39–54)

The readiness of some people to believe in Jesus at this stage of His ministry is illustrated in the rest of this chapter. How can a person believe?

1. *Through another's testimony* (verses 39, 40). 'It was hearing my mates talk about Christ that helped me most,' said a member of a youth club in London. Some of the Samaritans believed in Jesus because of the testimony of the Samaritan woman to what had impressed her about Him: 'He told me all that I ever did' (verse 39). There is real value in listening to the testimony of any ordinary Christian to the reality of Jesus Christ.

2. *Through the words of Jesus* (verses 41–54). The woman's testimony led many in her village to come to listen to Jesus Himself. The testimony of others should always lead us to find out more about it for ourselves by studying the words of Jesus, that is, the Bible. It is then that we are able to say: 'It is no longer because of your words that we believe, for we have *heard for ourselves*, and we know that this is indeed the Saviour of the world' (verse 42).

An illustration of faith (verses 46–54). The story of Jesus' return into Galilee, where John records the second 'sign', illustrates per-

47

fectly all we have been saying about the importance of faith resting on the words of Jesus. There must have been many in Galilee who thought of Jesus only as a wonder-worker. Hence Jesus' discouraging words to the official (and the crowd?), 'Unless you see signs and wonders you will not believe' (verse 48). The result of this interview with Jesus is that 'The man *believed the word* that Jesus spoke to him and went his way' (verse 50).

The official in this story was probably in the court of Herod the Tetrarch, with responsibilities comparable to those of a senior civil servant. He shows the extent of his faith in Jesus in (i) *being humble enough to ask for help*. He was in trouble. His much-loved son who had been ill for some time had taken a turn for the worse. It is common enough for a man to turn to God when in trouble. But this man did more than utter a prayer to God on the grounds that in trouble it is worth trying everything. He came, the courtier, to Jesus, the carpenter. He came humbly and sincerely without caring what others might think or say.

His faith also expressed itself in (ii) *being persistent enough to show he was serious*. Capernaum was almost twenty miles from Cana. It was a long way to come. But he showed he meant business. Jesus' first words to him were not encouraging (verse 48) but he determined to show that he was no trifler. The faith that Jesus rewards is persistent, persevering faith.

Again, this man demonstrated the reality of his faith in Jesus by (iii) *being confident enough to trust His words*. It was a long way to go to return home. But Jesus had promised: 'Go; your son will live.' Faith in Jesus is trusting His words, His promises. 'The man believed the word that Jesus spoke to him and went his way.'

Finally, this man proved the genuineness of his faith by (iv) *being willing to share it with others*. Confirmation of the truth of Jesus' words came later (verses 52, 53). His son was healed and he continued to believe in Jesus—*but so also did his household*, his family and slaves. No doubt it was not easy for him to share his faith with others. But genuine faith in Jesus always leads to this. Like the early Christians (Acts 4:20) the Christian believer 'cannot but speak of what (he has) seen and heard'. If we say we believe, it is worth asking whether we have ever told anyone else.

1 After this there was a feast of the Jews, and Jesus went up to Jerusalem.

2 Now there is in Jerusalem by the sheep gate a pool, in Hebrew called Bethzatha, which has five porticoes. [3]In these lay a multitude of invalids, blind, lame, paralysed, waiting for the moving of the water; [4]for an angel of the Lord went down at certain seasons into the pool, and troubled the water: whoever stepped in first after the troubling of the water was healed of whatever disease he had. [5]One man was there, who had been ill for thirty-eight years. [6]When Jesus saw him and knew that he had been lying there a long time, he said to him, 'Do you want to be healed?' [7]The sick man answered him, 'Sir, I have no man to put me into the pool when the water is troubled, and while I am going another steps down before me.' [8]Jesus said to him, 'Rise, take up your pallet, and walk.' [9]And at once the man was healed, and he took up his pallet and walked.

Now that day was the sabbath. [10]So the Jews said to the man who was cured, 'It is the sabbath, it is not lawful for you to carry your pallet.' [11]But he answered them, 'The man who healed me said to me, "Take up your pallet, and walk."' [12]They asked him, 'Who is the man who said to you, "Take up your pallet, and walk"?' [13]Now the man who had been healed did not know who it was, for Jesus had withdrawn, as there was a crowd in the place. [14]Afterward, Jesus found him in the temple, and said to him, 'See, you are well! Sin no more, that nothing worse befall you.' [15]The man went away and told the Jews that it was Jesus who had healed him. [16]And this was why the Jews persecuted Jesus, because he did this on the sabbath. [17]But Jesus answered them, 'My Father is working still, and I am working.' [18]This was why the Jews sought all the more to kill him, because he not only broke the sabbath but also called God his Father, making himself equal with God.

Jerusalem is the scene of this next incident which the writer describes. Many years ago it was thought impossible that a pool called Bethzatha (or, according to some manuscripts, Bethesda) with five porches or porticoes could have existed in Jerusalem.* However, excavations begun in 1876 near the Church of St. Anne in the north-east of the city revealed an ancient pool divided into two parts. There were four tall, roofed-in porticoes around the two sections of the pool and a fifth in between them. A faded fresco has also been discovered, representing the angel troubling the water, which makes it clear that, according to early Christian tradition, this was the place where our Lord healed the crippled man. A church was built on the spot as early as AD 480. Professor F. F. Bruce says, 'There are few sites in Jerusalem, mentioned in the Gospels, which can be identified so confidently.' †

This incident at Bethzatha provides an example of some common barriers to belief.

a. Personal unwillingness to believe

A man has been a cripple for thirty-eight years. There is a tradition that an angel comes from time to time to stir up the water and to convey healing to those who step into the pool. Year after year he lies near the pool, apparently without friends, and completely paralysed. No-one helps him until Jesus sees him. Jesus does not attack his superstitions but tries positively to help him exercise active faith in Himself. He tests his willingness to believe and says, 'Do you *want* to be healed?' This may seem a strange question. Yet it is easy for physical weakness, mental depression, a sense of hopelessness and despair to take away our willingness to *do* anything in such circumstances. We might even be unwilling to believe and obey someone who has the power to heal us completely.

I once asked a research student whether he would be willing to become a Christian if his intellectual objections were answered. He had the honesty to admit that he was *unwilling* to believe for other reasons. Jesus said on another occasion, 'If any man's will is to do his (God's) will, he shall know whether the teaching (of Jesus) is from God' (John 7:17). Sometimes man's greatest barrier to belief is his unwillingness to believe, however convincing the reasons for belief might be. The man in the story did not understand how

* See Introduction, p. 12.
† F. F. Bruce, *The New Testament Documents*, p. 94.

Jesus could help him; but when Jesus spoke to him he obeyed and was healed. He had overcome one barrier to belief.

b. Religious prejudice against belief

The cripple had not yet discovered a complete faith in Jesus. He did not know who Jesus was (verse 13). He had not yet realized that Jesus could save him from his sickness of heart as well as his sickness of body.

Afterwards Jesus found him in the Temple and was able to help him further. 'Sin no more,' He said, 'that nothing worse befall you' (verse 14). Jesus implies here that sometimes suffering is a consequence of sin, although elsewhere He makes it clear that this is not always so (see John 9). The man was well on the way to a firm faith in Jesus Christ.

But he had not bargained on the religious prejudice of some of the Jews. Sometimes religious people create serious barriers to belief for would-be disciples. The Jews had become legalistic about the sabbath. The Law had said that the sabbath day must be different from other days, and that on it neither a man nor his servants should work. The Jewish ecclesiastical leaders were not content with broad principles. They set out, for example, thirty-nine different classifications of work. The Rabbis solemnly argued that if a man carried a needle in his robe on the sabbath, or wore artificial teeth or a wooden leg, it could be 'work'. Certainly this man who was carrying his bed was working. The actual words were: 'If anyone carries anything from a public place to a private house on the sabbath intentionally, he is punishable by death by stoning.' No wonder the healed man tells the Jews that it is Jesus they want, not him. It looks as if religious men had once again hindered a man from finding and following the truth.

c. Hostility to Jesus

The writer here comments further and gives two reasons for the growing hostility of the religious bodies towards Jesus.

1. Because although Jesus kept the sabbath in principle—He worshipped in the synagogue, He served others, He probably rested

51

from some of the everyday activities—He ignored the petty rules and regulations imposed by the church of His day (verse 18).

2. Because Jesus claimed to be equal with God. When the Bible said that God rested on the seventh day, it meant, said Jesus, that He rested from one form of activity (creation) and continued in other activity. It did not mean that from that moment He ceased to be active in the affairs of men. 'God is active now,' said Jesus. 'My Father is working still, and I am working.' To the Jews these words made Jesus a blasphemer who was claiming to be equal with God, and therefore deserving of death (verse 18).

The real question is whether Jesus had a right to say such things. We, for our part, must be willing to obey the truth when we discover it; and we must be ready to distinguish between religious prejudice and religious principle. If we do not we shall find ourselves diverted from the truth or even hostile to it.

11 THE CLAIMS OF JESUS
5:19–29

19 Jesus said to them, 'Truly, truly, I say to you, the Son can do nothing of his own accord, but only what he sees the Father doing; for whatever he does, that the Son does likewise. 20For the Father loves the Son, and shows him all that he himself is doing; and greater works than these will he show him, that you may marvel. 21For as the Father raises the dead and gives them life, so also the Son gives life to whom he will. 22The Father judges no one, but has given all judgment to the Son, 23that all may honour the Son, even as they honour the Father. He who does not honour the Son does not honour the Father who sent him. 24Truly, truly, I say to you, he who hears my word and believes him who sent me, has eternal life; he does not come into judgment, but has passed from death to life.

25 'Truly, truly, I say to you, the hour is coming, and now is, when the dead will hear the voice of the Son of God, and those

who hear will live. ²⁶For as the Father has life in himself, so he has granted the Son also to have life in himself, ²⁷and has given him authority to execute judgment, because he is the Son of man. ²⁸Do not marvel at this; for the hour is coming when all who are in the tombs will hear his voice ²⁹and come forth, those who have done good, to the resurrection of life, and those who have done evil, to the resurrection of judgment.'

In a recent study of religion and religious education as seen by 400 third-year students at Oxford, Cambridge and Bangor* the following statistics were enumerated: 28 per cent of the students called themselves convinced and practising members of Christian churches. Eleven per cent believed in the divinity of Christ, but were not committed to any particular church. Twenty per cent could not accept the divinity of Christ, but were prepared to accept His ethical teaching. Twenty-eight per cent were agnostic, and 13 per cent were agnostic or atheist and regretted that so many people were misled by religion.

It may surprise us that so large a minority of students accepted the divinity of Christ. It is not at all clear, of course, how many understood the implications of such a belief. But it is clear that many cannot accept the Christian claim that Jesus is divine, any more than that many of the Jews could accept it in His own day. No-one needs to pretend that such a claim is easy to understand. The late Professor C. S. Lewis once wrote: 'If Christianity was something we were making up, of course we could make it easier. But it isn't. We can't compete, in simplicity, with people who are inventing religions. How could we? We're dealing with fact. Of course anyone can be simple if he has no facts to bother about.' But if we are prepared to grapple with this next passage we shall see how Jesus understands His own unique relationship to His Father, and the extravagance of His claims.

a. Jesus claims that He is dependent on God (verse 19)

The words 'truly, truly' are always used for emphasis in John's Gospel. Jesus wanted to emphasize His dependence upon God in His human life. 'The Son can do nothing of his own accord, but only what he sees the Father doing.' All who believe in God would

* R. J. Rees, *Background and Belief.*

want to acknowledge their dependence upon Him. But none of us could go on to say, as Jesus did, 'for whatever he does, that the Son does likewise.' Jesus' dependence upon God is a perfect dependence. Expressed positively, He explained it in His own words when He said, 'I always do what is pleasing to him (the Father)' (John 8:29). Is He mad, bad, or God, to make such a claim?

b. Jesus claims that He is equal with God (verses 20–29)

For (see verse 19 again) 'whatever he (the Father) does, that the Son does likewise'. Jesus claims equality with God by announcing that He shares the rights and powers of God Himself.

1. *By doing the works of God* (verse 20). When Nicodemus met Jesus (see John 3) he said to Him, 'No one can do these signs that you do, unless God is with him.' Jesus goes further than this: 'The Father loves the Son, and shows him all that he himself is doing; and greater works than these will he show him.' Jesus not only knows that God is working *with* Him. He knows perfectly all that the Father is doing in the world through Him. Jesus speaks here of a uniquely close relationship with God, the heavenly Father.

2. *By giving eternal life* (verse 21). Surely only God has the power to give eternal life, and to raise men from the dead? God alone is the source of life. Jesus claims these rights.

3. *By judging men* (verse 22). The Jew believed that God alone is the judge of all men. God alone knows our hearts and motives. The Jew believed that there would be a climax to history, and that God would judge all men. This authority to judge, Jesus claims for Himself. 'The Father judges no one, but has given all judgment to the Son.' Who is this peasant preacher who can make such a claim?

4. *By accepting man's honour* (verse 23). Humility is a virtue that we expect to find in great saints and religious leaders. This claim of Jesus to have an equal right with God to receive the honour of men is utter conceit, unless Jesus was indeed equal with God. Jesus claims that to honour Him is to honour God, and to dishonour Him is to dishonour God. When a man says I believe in God, but I cannot accept Jesus, he is, according to Jesus, dishonouring and ignoring God Himself. Is this conceit or sober truth?

5. *By settling man's destiny* (verses 24–29). No mere man,

however great, would claim to settle the eternal destiny of another unless he was suffering from delusions or megalomania. But Jesus claims with great emphasis that a man's attitude to His own words, as well as his faith in God, settles his present enjoyment of spiritual life now (the Greek tense suggests that a believer in Jesus *already has* eternal life), as well as his destiny in the future (verse 24).

Jesus goes on to use two titles to describe Himself. He is the unique *Son of God*. Those who hear His voice *now* and respond to Him will live. They will come alive spiritually. They will recognize that God is speaking to them. He also claims to be the *Son of man*. In the Old Testament book of Daniel the prophet sees a vision of a divine figure, called the Son of man, coming in the clouds in judgment (see Daniel 7:13, 14). Jesus claims to be the Son of man. He will execute judgment. If Jesus is merely a man, a prophet, an outstanding teacher, then we need not take this claim seriously. Indeed any man who claims to do the works of God, to give eternal life, to judge sinners, to accept honour due to God and to settle a man's destiny, must be either deluded or divine. The one thing He cannot be is just a good man. No mere man in his senses could make claims like this. Only God Himself has the right to make such claims. If Jesus is God, then these words are serious indeed. It is God who has come to tell us that there are two possible destinies for each of us—the resurrection to life or the resurrection to judgment (verses 28, 29). *Who, then, is Jesus Christ?* Is He deluded or divine?

12 THE AUTHORITY OF JESUS
5:30–47

30 'I can do nothing on my own authority; as I hear, I judge; and my judgment is just, because I seek not my own will but the will of him who sent me. [31]If I bear witness to myself, my

testimony is not true; ³²there is another who bears witness to me, and I know that the testimony which he bears to me is true. ³³You sent to John, and he has borne witness to the truth. ³⁴Not that the testimony which I receive is from man; but I say this that you may be saved. ³⁵He was a burning and shining lamp, and you were willing to rejoice for a while in his light. ³⁶But the testimony which I have is greater than that of John; for the works which the Father has granted me to accomplish, these very works which I am doing, bear me witness that the Father has sent me. ³⁷And the Father who sent me has himself borne witness to me. His voice you have never heard, his form you have never seen; ³⁸and you do not have his word abiding in you, for you do not believe him whom he has sent. ³⁹You search the scriptures, because you think that in them you have eternal life; and it is they that bear witness to me; ⁴⁰yet you refuse to come to me that you may have life. ⁴¹I do not receive glory from men. ⁴²But I know that you have not the love of God within you. ⁴³I have come in my Father's name, and you do not receive me; if another comes in his own name, him you will receive. ⁴⁴How can you believe, who receive glory from one another and do not seek the glory that comes from the only God? ⁴⁵Do not think that I shall accuse you to the Father; it is Moses who accuses you, on whom you set your hope. ⁴⁶If you believed Moses, you would believe me, for he wrote of me. ⁴⁷But if you do not believe his writings, how will you believe my words?'

The question of authority is crucial in religion. We have considered some of the claims of Jesus, making Himself equal with God. The vital question is, 'On what authority does He make such claims?' Or, to put it another way, 'In what way does He substantiate such stupendous statements about Himself?' Jesus makes it clear in His teaching that He is not 'another God'. He is not independent of His heavenly Father (verse 30). So, as He argues with the critical Jewish leaders about His own authority, He brings forward His witnesses.

a. The witness of His Father (verse 32)

'There is another who bears witness to me, and I know that the testimony which he bears to me is true.' The true witness of the Father to Jesus' unique Sonship to which Jesus refers here seems to be the occasion of Jesus' baptism (John 1:29-34). But the Jewish

glory—

or the actions by which He manifested his

leaders, unwilling to be baptized by John the Baptist, failed to hear or see God's witness to Jesus on that occasion (verse 37). For those who were looking for the Messiah, and longing for His coming, God had not been silent in witnessing to the truth about Jesus.

b. The witness of John the Baptist (verses 33–35)

He too witnessed to the truth about Christ. John the Baptist was admired by the Jews for his single-mindedness and courage. Here was a man who spoke the truth even at risk to his life. He was a great personality and 'a burning and shining lamp', and could easily have taken away a large following of disciples for himself. But he always pointed to Jesus as the Messiah, and acknowledged that Jesus was the Son of God (John 1:34). If the Jews had only listened to John the Baptist they would have acknowledged Jesus and would have been saved from the inevitable judgment that would follow their rejection of the Messiah (verse 34).

c. The witness of the works of Jesus

The Jews ought to have recognized that the 'works' or 'miracles' which Jesus did were 'signs' to them that God's Messiah had come. The Old Testament prophets had looked forward to a day when the Messiah, who was to be the agent of all God's purposes in the world, would come to His people. He was described significantly as Emmanuel, *God with us* (Isaiah 7:14). He would be called 'Wonderful Counsellor, *Mighty God*, Everlasting Father, Prince of Peace' (Isaiah 9:6). One sign of His coming would be that He would preach good news to the poor, bind up the broken-hearted, proclaim release to the captives and recovering of sight to the blind, and set at liberty those who are oppressed (see Isaiah 61:1, 2; Luke 4:16–21). There was a time when John the Baptist in a fit of depression almost lost his faith in Jesus. Jesus reminded John of the 'works' He was doing, in fulfilment of the Old Testament, as an answer to the question, 'Are you he who is to come, or shall we look for another?' (Luke 7:18–22). The Jewish leaders ought to have seen in the 'works' and miracles of Jesus a witness to His authority, and a sign that He was indeed from God.

d. The witness of the Scriptures (verse 39)

We have noticed already how the Old Testament Scriptures pointed to Jesus. '*It is they that bear witness to me.*' When Jesus spoke with the disciples on the Emmaus road after the resurrection (Luke 24) 'he interpreted to them in all the scriptures (that is, the Old Testament as we know it) the things concerning himself' (verse 27). The Jews did well to search the Scriptures, for in them they might indeed find eternal life. But the Scriptures are a signpost that points to Jesus Christ. They are not Christ Himself. It is possible, for us to make the same mistake as the Jews. We can read about the Christ of the Bible, but never come to the Christ of the Bible. 'The Bible bears witness to me,' says Jesus, 'but you refuse to *come to me* that you may have life.' It is not enough to read the Bible. We must obey the Bible and come to Jesus Christ Himself. In Him alone is eternal life.

e. The witnesses rejected

Why did so many of the Jews refuse this witness to Jesus Christ? Jesus gave these answers.

1. *Their love for God was formal* (verses 41, 42). They said they loved God, but their hearts were unmoved. Religion to many of them was only a form, an outward façade.

2. *Their consideration of Christ was superficial* (verse 43). They accepted the claims of other men sometimes with no evidence as to their genuineness. But they would not consider the witness of God to the claims of Jesus. I am always amazed at the way men will accept, say, the arguments for Mormonism, or flying saucers, or re-incarnation, on the slenderest of evidence and never consider the weighty evidence for the deity of Christ.

3. *Their acknowledgment of God was hypocritical* (verse 44). They pretended that they wanted God to be honoured in their lives. In reality they wanted the praise and honour of their friends. They regarded man's honour as more important than God's praise. Many a man has turned his back upon God because of his fear that he would lose the good opinion of men.

4. *Their knowledge of the Scriptures was theoretical* (verses 46, 47). They said they believed in the writings of Moses. They set

their hope on him. They memorized many of his words. They even taught others what he said. But they did not act on what he said. They showed therefore that they did not really take the Old Testament seriously. If they claimed to believe Moses in theory, but failed in practice, how unlikely it would be that they would act on the words of Jesus, when they would not believe His claims. Christian belief is more than theoretical assent to certain propositions in the Bible. It is practical experimental trust in the living Jesus Christ to whom the Scriptures witness.

Christ's authority rests on God Himself. God has vouched for that divine authority through men (*e.g.* John the Baptist), through miracles and through the Scriptures. However, *a person will never be convinced of His authority until he is willing to submit to it, and humbly come to Jesus.*

13 THE POWER OF JESUS
6:1–24

1 After this Jesus went to the other side of the sea of Galilee, which is the sea of Tiberias. ²And a multitude followed him, because they saw the signs which he did on those who were diseased. ³Jesus went up into the hills, and there sat down with his disciples. ⁴Now the Passover, the feast of the Jews, was at hand. ⁵Lifting up his eyes, then, and seeing that a multitude was coming to him, Jesus said to Philip, 'How are we to buy bread, so that these people may eat?' ⁶This he said to test him, for he himself knew what he would do. ⁷Philip answered him, 'Two hundred denarii would not buy enough bread for each of them to get a little.' ⁸One of his disciples, Andrew, Simon Peter's brother, said to him, ⁹'There is a lad here who has five barley loaves and two fish; but what are they among so many?' ¹⁰Jesus said, 'Make the people sit down.' Now there was much grass in the place; so the men sat down, in number about five thousand. ¹¹Jesus then took the loaves, and when he had given thanks, he distributed them to those who were seated;

so also the fish, as much as they wanted. ¹²And when they had eaten their fill, he told his disciples, 'Gather up the fragments left over, that nothing may be lost.' ¹³So they gathered them up and filled twelve baskets with fragments from the five barley loaves, left by those who had eaten. ¹⁴When the people saw the sign which he had done, they said, 'This is indeed the prophet who is to come into the world!'

15 Perceiving then that they were about to come and take him by force to make him king, Jesus withdrew again to the hills by himself.

16 When evening came, his disciples went down to the sea, ¹⁷got into a boat, and started across the sea to Capernaum. It was now dark, and Jesus had not yet come to them. ¹⁸The sea rose because a strong wind was blowing. ¹⁹When they had rowed about three or four miles, they saw Jesus walking on the sea and drawing near to the boat. They were frightened, ²⁰but he said to them, 'It is I; do not be afraid.' ²¹Then they were glad to take him into the boat, and immediately the boat was at the land to which they were going.

22 On the next day the people who remained on the other side of the sea saw that there had been only one boat there, and that Jesus had not entered the boat with his disciples, but that his disciples had gone away alone. ²³However, boats from Tiberias came near the place where they ate the bread after the Lord had given thanks. ²⁴So when the people saw that Jesus was not there, nor his disciples, they themselves got into the boats and went to Capernaum, seeking Jesus.

The two incidents in this passage show us the authority and power of Jesus in action. It was not only in what Jesus said (His claims) but in what He did (His works) that we understand His power and deity. He always practised what He preached.

a. The feeding of the five thousand (verses 1–15)

The narrative describes an act of superhuman power. Five loaves and two fishes taken into the hands of Jesus, then broken and distributed, feed about five thousand people. Twelve baskets are then filled with the scraps that are left over. Someone has said that the example of the boy handing over his picnic lunch to Jesus led all the others to bring out their food too and to share it so that there was enough for all. That is very ingenious, but it is not what the writer describes. Here again an estimate of Jesus Christ Himself will determine our view of the likelihood of such a miracle (see note on John 2).

We could add to this argument the fact that early non-Christian writers who refer to Jesus at any length do not dispute that He performed miracles. Josephus called Him a 'wonder-worker'. Other Jewish Rabbis attribute His miracles to sorcery. Celsus, the second-century critic of Christianity, also attributed them to the power of sorcery, but these writers do not deny that they happened!* We ought to remember too that the apostles in the early church refer to the miracles of Jesus as facts which no-one would dispute (Acts 2:22) and some of the early Christian apologists refer to them as events beyond dispute by the critics of Christianity.†

Jesus had no doubt welcomed the escape with His disciples to the solitude of the hills after the hectic days in Galilee. But it was not long before the crowds, including some of the pilgrims who were on their way to the Passover festival, heard where He was and came swarming up the hillside to see Him (verses 1–5).

Jesus' question to Philip was partly a sign of His concern for the people, and partly a way of testing Philip's faith: 'How are we to buy bread, so that these people may eat?' (verses 5, 6). Did Philip know Jesus well enough to believe He could do something about this situation? Philip was down to earth, practical and unimaginative as ever. A quick reckoning showed him that it would take more than six months' wages to buy enough food to feed this crowd! (A denarius was the standard day's wage for a working man.) It was just not an economic proposition. I sometimes wonder how often the church of Jesus Christ has failed to see the power of Christ at work for the same reasons.

Andrew's suggestion is also half-hearted, and he probably felt slightly ridiculous in making it. 'There is a lad here who has five barley loaves and two fish; but what are they among so many?' But it is precisely with the picnic lunch of a young lad, willingly given, that Jesus demonstrates His power to satisfy the needs of the crowd. Small things, small gifts, in the hands of Jesus can often be a source

* Origen, *Against Celsus*, i. 38; ii. 48.
† *E.g.* Quadratus, in his Apologies addressed to the Emperor Hadrian in AD 133 (Eusebius, *Ecclesiastical History*, iv. 3).

of power and help to others. Furthermore, Jesus never does things in half measures (see verse 13).

When the people saw the sign which He had done they said, 'This is indeed *the* prophet who is to come into the world!' (verse 14). They recognized this amazing miracle as a sign that Jesus was the long-expected Messiah, or King (verse 15). The crowd did not yet understand the kind of King He would be, so that Jesus had to slip away quietly (verse 15). But they were beginning to see that you cannot explain Jesus completely by saying 'He is just a good man'.

b. Jesus walking on the lake (verses 16–21)
  (*cf.* Matthew 14:22–27; Mark 6:45–51)

Jesus now gives the disciples further opportunity to understand who He is and to exercise faith in Him. One of the sudden storms that often descends on the lake causes the disciples great distress as, without Jesus, they row across the sea to Capernaum. They toss about on the waves. For three or four miles they row desperately. Although they are experienced sailors, they begin to be terrified. Suddenly Jesus appears, walking on the water. He is not only Lord of the harvest, but Lord of the elements as well. To some Jewish minds the water in a lake is the place of evil spirits. The deity of Jesus assures us that He is Lord and Sovereign over all. As the Negro spiritual has it: 'He's got the whole world in His hands.' So Jesus can say 'It is I; do not be afraid'.

In Mark's account (Mark 6:45–51) we are told that when Jesus got into the boat 'the wind ceased. And they were utterly astounded, *for they did not understand about the loaves*, but their hearts were hardened'. This must have been their first reaction. We find it hard to believe at first that Jesus is as powerful as this, especially when we have just discovered our own weakness and inadequacy in a situation in which we are supposed to be experts. The disciples were *skilled* fishermen! Jesus often comes to us even when we fail in our strong points, and says, 'It is I; do not be afraid.' We may at first harden our hearts, like the disciples. However, we learn from Matthew's Gospel (Matthew 14:22–27) that those in the boat later worshipped Him, saying, 'Truly you are the Son of God.' They were beginning to understand, by considering His works, who Jesus really was.

Many people are discouraged because they *feel* they have so little faith, especially in times of failure and fear. The New Testament encourages us to believe that it is not the *amount* of faith that matters most but the *direction* of it. My faith may be as small as a grain of mustard seed, but if it is centred on Jesus Christ and a growing understanding of who He is, it will become living and strong. The Christian believes that Jesus Christ is in control of all things. So he is not afraid.

14 JESUS AND THE SEEKER
6:25–40

25 When they found him on the other side of the sea, they said to him, 'Rabbi, when did you come here?' ²⁶Jesus answered them, 'Truly, truly, I say to you, you seek me, not because you saw signs, but because you ate your fill of the loaves. ²⁷Do not labour for the food which perishes, but for the food which endures to eternal life, which the Son of man will give to you; for on him has God the Father set his seal.' ²⁸Then they said to him, 'What must we do, to be doing the work of God?' ²⁹Jesus answered them, 'This is the work of God, that you believe in him whom he has sent.' ³⁰So they said to him, 'Then what sign do you do, that we may see, and believe you? What work do you perform? ³¹Our fathers ate the manna in the wilderness; as it is written, "He gave them bread from heaven to eat."' ³²Jesus then said to them, 'Truly, truly, I say to you, it was not Moses who gave you the bread from heaven; my Father gives you the true bread from heaven. ³³For the bread of God is that which comes down from heaven, and gives life to the world.' ³⁴They said to him, 'Lord, give us this bread always.'

35 Jesus said to them, 'I am the bread of life; he who comes to me shall not hunger, and he who believes in me shall never thirst. ³⁶But I said to you that you have seen me and yet do not

believe. ³⁷All that the Father gives me will come to me; and him who comes to me I will not cast out. ³⁸For I have come down from heaven, not to do my own will, but the will of him who sent me; ³⁹and this is the will of him who sent me, that I should lose nothing of all that he has given me, but raise it up at the last day. ⁴⁰For this is the will of my Father, that every one who sees the Son and believes in him should have eternal life; and I will raise him up at the last day.'

Although many will not acknowledge the deity of Jesus or His claims upon their lives, there are few who have not been drawn in some way by the attractiveness of Jesus Christ. Charles Lamb, the writer, once said: 'If Shakespeare was to come into the room, we should all rise up to meet him; but if that Person (Jesus) was to come into it, we should all fall down and try to kiss the hem of His garment.'* Here in this story in John's Gospel we find crowds of ordinary people, not really understanding who Jesus is, or what He came to do, 'seeking Jesus' (verse 24), attracted by Him.

However, this narrative makes it clear that if we are to find the satisfaction and life that Jesus can give us, we must come to Him with some understanding of who He is and what He comes to do, and what He offers and demands. The answers Jesus gives to certain questions that are put to Him help us to understand how we may approach Him.

a. The questions of the crowd

1. *'Rabbi, when did you come here?'* (verses 25–27). Jesus saw this as a polite opening gambit. He does not answer this unimportant question, but speaks instead of *why they had come to Him*. Our motives for seeking Jesus are important. These men came to Jesus for what they could get out of Him. They came hoping for material gain and physical satisfaction. They saw Jesus possibly as the answer to their economic problems, and as one who would raise their standard of living. Jesus does not promise us material prosperity if we follow Him, or physical and material comforts, nor should we expect advance in social status. We may well find the opposite is true. But He does not turn us away if we seek

* Quoted by P. Carnegie Simpson in *The Fact of Christ*, p. 22.

Him at first with false or mixed motives. He merely helps us to see that spiritual satisfaction is more important than physical (though His feeding of the five thousand shows that He is not unconcerned about man's physical need, and the starving millions). Our greatest effort should be given to discovering that spiritual food which leads to eternal life. This food is to be found in Jesus Christ. For God Himself, in giving Him power to feed 5,000, has set His seal on Him, and marked Him out as God's answer to man's need.

2. *'What must we do, to be doing the work of God?'* (verse 28). This question again uncovers the way that most of us first approach God's offer of life and satisfaction in Jesus Christ. 'What must we *do?'* 'What works must we perform?' Does Jesus require more prayers, more church-going, more deeds of mercy, more kind actions? In our hearts we all think like the Jews here, 'What must we do, to be doing the work of God?' There is of course something to do. But it is nothing we can achieve. It is nothing that earns us the right to new life in Jesus Christ. Jesus said, 'This is the work of God, *that you believe in him* whom he has sent.' It is not achieving anything that saves me, but believing, trusting in Jesus.

3. *'What sign do you do, that we may see, and believe you? What work do you perform?'* (verse 30). Men say, 'Seeing is believing.' The Jews said, 'We must have proof. Moses was a great leader because he provided food for the Israelites in the wilderness. What proof do you give us that you are greater than he is?' It was a natural question. This Gospel goes on to show us that a deeper faith can say 'believing is seeing'. But the answer Jesus gives provides sufficient grounds for a firm belief.

(i) He corrects their argument. Moses had not given bread (or manna, as it was called) to the Israelites. *God* had provided it, and met the physical needs of the Jews at that time. This bread saved their lives.

(ii) God likewise has provided the true Bread from heaven, because Jesus has come from heaven into the world. In Jesus all men may find their spiritual needs met. He gives life to all.

(iii) In answer to their request 'Lord, give us this bread always', Jesus explains more exactly what He means. He says, 'I am the bread of life.' Bread is the staff of life; without it we cannot live. Jesus is the source of spiritual life; without Him we cannot live.

Bread satisfies for a time. Jesus will satisfy always. Those who are hungry and thirsty of heart will find complete satisfaction in Jesus Christ.

b. The mystery of God's actions (verses 36–40)

Why is it that some men do not come to Jesus even when they know something about Him (verse 36)? Jesus' answer uncovers a mystery which the finite mind of man has never fully understood. For when a man comes to Christ two complementary truths can be recognized in his experience.

1. *God the Father gives the man to Christ.* 'All that the Father *gives* me will come to me' (*cf.* verses 38, 39). Every Christian knows that he is a Christian only because of the working of God the Father in his life. God took the initiative. God was in control of the circumstances. God laid hold on us before we lay hold on Him. God spoke to us before we spoke to God. He loved us before we began to love Him. Furthermore, once God has given us to Christ, we know that it is God's will to keep us and to raise us up on the last day. 'For this is the will of my Father, that every one who sees the Son and believes in him should have eternal life; and I will raise him up at the last day' (verse 40). Once God has given me to Jesus Christ, I am eternally secure in Him.

2. *A man must come to God the Son and believe.* The previous truth about God's sovereignty does not lessen the importance of man's responsibility. It is 'him who *comes* to me', says Jesus, 'I will not cast out' (verse 37). It is *everyone* who 'sees the Son and *believes* in him' who has eternal life (verse 40). Moreover, it is possible to see who He is and to understand what He came to do with the eye of faith.

The late Professor C. S. Lewis has described this paradoxical and existential experience in his own inimitable way. 'The odd thing was that before God closed in on me, I was in fact offered what now appears a moment of wholly free choice. In a sense I was going up Headington Hill on the top of a bus. Without words and (I think) almost without images, a fact about myself was somehow presented to me. I became aware that I was holding something at bay, or shutting something out. Or if you like that I was wearing some stiff clothing, like corsets, or even a suit of armour, as if I were a lobster. I felt myself being, there and then, given a free choice. I could open the door or keep it shut. I could unbuckle the armour or keep it on. Neither choice was presented as a duty: no threat or promise was attached to either, though I knew that to open the door or to take off the corslet meant the incalculable. The choice appeared to be momentous but it was also strongly un-emotional. I was moved by no desires or fears. In a sense I was not moved by anything. I chose to open, to unbuckle, to loosen the rein. I chose, yet it did not really seem possible to do the opposite.'*

God never forces a man to be a Christian. He has given us the precious gift of free will. He respects that gift. We must come to Him and believe. But when we have come we know it is the work of God. When we have believed we know it is the gift of God.

15 THE CHALLENGE OF PERSONAL FAITH
6:41-71

41 The Jews then murmured at him, because he said, 'I am the bread which came down from heaven.' 42They said, 'Is not this Jesus, the son of Joseph, whose father and mother we know? How does he now say, "I have come down from heaven"?' 43Jesus answered them, 'Do not murmur among yourselves. 44No one can come to me unless the Father who sent me draws him; and I will raise him up at the last day. 45It is written in the prophets, "And they shall all be taught by God." Every one who has heard and learned from the Father comes to me. 46Not that any one has seen the Father except him who is from God; he has seen the Father. 47Truly, truly, I say to you, he who believes has eternal life. 48I am the bread of life. 49Your fathers ate the manna in the wilderness, and they died. 50This is the bread which comes down from heaven, that a man may eat of it and not die. 51I am the living bread which came down

* C. S. Lewis, *Surprised by Joy*, p. 211.

from heaven; if any one eats of this bread, he will live for ever; and the bread which I shall give for the life of the world is my flesh.'

52 The Jews then disputed among themselves, saying, 'How can this man give us his flesh to eat?' [53]So Jesus said to them, 'Truly, truly, I say to you, unless you eat the flesh of the Son of man and drink his blood, you have no life in you; [54]he who eats my flesh and drinks my blood has eternal life, and I will raise him up at the last day. [55]For my flesh is food indeed, and my blood is drink indeed. [56]He who eats my flesh and drinks my blood abides in me, and I in him. [57]As the living Father sent me, and I live because of the Father, so he who eats me will live because of me. [58]This is the bread which came down from heaven, not such as the fathers ate and died; he who eats this bread will live for ever.' [59]This he said in the synagogue, as he taught at Capernaum.

60 Many of his disciples, when they heard it, said, 'This is a hard saying; who can listen to it?' [61]But Jesus, knowing in himself that his disciples murmured at it, said to them, 'Do you take offence at this? [62]Then what if you were to see the Son of man ascending where he was before? [63]It is the spirit that gives life, the flesh is of no avail; the words that I have spoken to you are spirit and life. [64]But there are some of you that do not believe.' For Jesus knew from the first who those were that did not believe, and who it was that should betray him. [65]And he said, 'This is why I told you that no one can come to me unless it is granted him by the Father.'

66 After this many of his disciples drew back and no longer went about with him. [67]Jesus said to the twelve, 'Will you also go away?' [68]Simon Peter answered him, 'Lord, to whom shall we go? You have the words of eternal life; [69]and we have believed, and have come to know, that you are the Holy One of God.' [70]Jesus answered them, 'Did I not choose you, the twelve, and one of you is a devil?' [71]He spoke of Judas the son of Simon Iscariot, for he, one of the twelve, was to betray him.

One of the most astonishing lessons of history is the way in which clever men, sometimes religious men, have found ways of denigrating Jesus Christ as soon as His demands have been made clear and personal. Indeed it is because Jesus Christ makes religion so personal that many draw back from it. When Jesus speaks of 'coming to Me' and 'believing on Me' it is too simple, we say. We mean it is too personal and demanding. In the rest of this chapter we see the excuses that some religious men made when confronted with the Person of Jesus Christ Himself.

a. They denied His claim to be divine (verses 41–51)

They sneered at His earthly home. The Jews disagreed with Jesus' claim to be 'the bread which came down from heaven'. They recognized this as a claim to deity. Jesus was not simply born into the world: *He came from heaven.* But, His critics said, we know this man's parents, Joseph and Mary. He comes from a carpenter's home, and from Nazareth, of all disreputable places! Would God come from such humble stock, and in such a humble manner?

Jesus' answer points out that their very objection shows how little they know God, for all their boasting to be religious. If they knew the voice of God, they would acknowledge the words of Christ (verse 45). He also reiterates the point that unless the Father draws them they will not come to Him (verse 44). However, Jesus does not deny their charge, but simply restates His own claims (see verses 44, 45, 46, 47, 50, 51). We are already familiar with His claims to raise up believers at the Last Day, to give eternal life and satisfaction. But Jesus now includes a deeper truth. 'The bread which I shall give for the life of the world is my flesh' (verse 51). Jesus now teaches that eternal life and satisfaction is made possible only by His death—by giving His flesh, or by laying down His life for the world.

b. They denied His teaching about death (verses 52–58)

They sneered at its crudity. There is no denying that the words of Jesus concerning the giving of His own body in death are crude and difficult to understand. There is something even more crude and terrible about the crucifixion of Jesus Christ which the writer of this Gospel sees as 'the hour', the great moment, of the ministry of Jesus. Jesus did not die on a beautiful gilded cross such as we see in some churches; but on a rough-hewn tree, knocked into the shape of a cross.

Quite apart from the crudity of the idea, what did Jesus mean by *'eating His flesh and drinking His blood'*? Even His disciples found this hard to understand and offensive to their ears (verses 60, 61). Jesus explained this in a sermon in the synagogue at Capernaum (verses 52–59), and possibly privately to His disciples as well (verses 60–71). The two main points stand out.

1. *The importance of a personal appropriation of Christ Himself.*
If you gave a starving man a lecture on the chemical properties of
bread, or held up a poster depicting the satisfying nature of a
wholemeal loaf, it would not help to satisfy the poor man at all. A
hungry man needs to take food and eat it. He cannot live unless he
eats.

So it is not enough to hear about Jesus Christ, or to analyse His
nature, or to believe certain facts about Him, or simply to read about
Him. Spiritual satisfaction and life is given only when we take
Him and personally appropriate or receive Him for ourselves. We
take Him as God become man (the Bread from heaven). We take
Him as the Saviour of sinners (flesh and blood *given* for the life of
the world, verse 51). When we receive Jesus as Son of God and
Saviour of sinners personally into our lives, we may be said to eat
His flesh and drink His blood. He then lives in us, and we in Him,
in close union and friendship (verse 56). He then continues to sustain us spiritually as we continue to believe on Him, and draw
strength and life from Him (see John 15). A friend of mine, a research graduate from Ceylon, wrote this about his search for the
truth in the Gospels. 'As I read the Gospels there was a growing
awareness in my mind that a Person stood out of the pages, and
He seemed alive. The historical Jesus became very immediate. I
knelt and prayed, perhaps for the first time sincerely, and asked
Jesus to forgive my sins and come into my life. I can say quite
honestly that moment proved to be very decisive in my life. . . .
From that day onwards the Lord Jesus Christ has proved to be my
Saviour, Friend and Companion through all walks of life.' He had
received Jesus personally by faith.

2. *The importance of a right interpretation of Christ's teaching.*
The disciples who found this teaching of Jesus offensive had failed
to understand the spiritual significance of what Jesus was saying.
They failed to understand that Jesus often spoke of spiritual truths
in material terms. Clearly Jesus did not mean that they must literally
eat His actual flesh and blood if they were to know eternal life. As
Jesus said, 'It is the spirit that gives life, the flesh is of no avail; *the
words that I have spoken to you are spirit and life*' (verse 63). Those
who use these words to endorse the view of some Christians that
at the Holy Communion service the bread and wine is changed into

the actual body and blood of Christ are surely making the same mistake as the disciples here. When Jesus speaks of the Son of man ascending to heaven (verse 62), perhaps He is suggesting that when this happens they will understand better the spiritual significance of these words (*cf.* John 16:7). It is as the Spirit of God applies the words of Christ to us that we are able spiritually to feed on Christ in our hearts by faith.

Men often find it easier to worship God in a material form than in a spiritual manner. Idolatry in the Old Testament was an example of this. Priestcraft and ritual in all religions endorse this view. Even Judas, the disciple who later betrayed Jesus, found the material advantage of betraying Jesus (thirty pieces of silver) at first more satisfying than the spiritual gain of following Him. If spiritual life is possible only through the physical death of Jesus, then what sort of Messiah, what sort of King was He? What sort of life was He offering them? We are not surprised to find that 'after this many of his disciples drew back and no longer went about with him' (verse 66). Would His special followers, the twelve disciples, also leave Him at this point in His mission? Simon Peter's answer to the question 'Will you also go away?' is a good one to turn over in our own minds (see verses 68, 69).

16 GROWING OPPOSITION
7:1–31

1 After this Jesus went about in Galilee; he would not go about in Judea, because the Jews sought to kill him. ²Now the Jews' feast of Tabernacles was at hand. ³So his brothers said to him, 'Leave here and go to Judea, that your disciples may see the works you are doing. ⁴For no man works in secret if he seeks to be known openly. If you do these things, show yourself to the world.' ⁵For even his brothers did not believe in him. ⁶Jesus said to them, 'My time has not yet come, but your time

is always here. ⁷The world cannot hate you, but it hates me because I testify of it that its works are evil. ⁸Go to the feast yourselves; I am not going up to the feast, for my time has not yet fully come.' ⁹So saying, he remained in Galilee.

10 But after his brothers had gone up to the feast, then he also went up, not publicly but in private. ¹¹The Jews were looking for him at the feast, and saying, 'Where is he?' ¹²And there was much muttering about him among the people. While some said, 'He is a good man,' others said, 'No, he is leading the people astray.' ¹³Yet for fear of the Jews no one spoke openly of him.

14 About the middle of the feast Jesus went up into the temple and taught. ¹⁵The Jews marvelled at it, saying, 'How is it that this man has learning, when he has never studied?' ¹⁶So Jesus answered them, 'My teaching is not mine, but his who sent me; ¹⁷if any man's will is to do his will, he shall know whether the teaching is from God or whether I am speaking on my own authority. ¹⁸He who speaks on his own authority seeks his own glory; but he who seeks the glory of him who sent him is true, and in him there is no falsehood. ¹⁹Did not Moses give you the law? Yet none of you keeps the law. Why do you seek to kill me?' ²⁰The people answered, 'You have a demon! Who is seeking to kill you?' ²¹Jesus answered them, 'I did one deed, and you all marvel at it. ²²Moses gave you circumcision (not that it is from Moses, but from the fathers), and you circumcise a man upon the sabbath. ²³If on the sabbath a man receives circumcision, so that the law of Moses may not be broken, are you angry with me because on the sabbath I made a man's whole body well? ²⁴Do not judge by appearances, but judge with right judgment.'

25 Some of the people of Jerusalem therefore said, 'Is not this the man whom they seek to kill? ²⁶And here he is, speaking openly, and they say nothing to him! Can it be that the authorities really know that this is the Christ? ²⁷Yet we know where this man comes from; and when the Christ appears, no one will know where he comes from.' ²⁸So Jesus proclaimed, as he taught in the temple, 'You know me, and you know where I come from? But I have not come of my own accord; he who sent me is true, and him you do not know. ²⁹I know him, for I come from him, and he sent me.' ³⁰So they sought to arrest him; but no one laid hands on him, because his hour had not yet come. ³¹Yet many of the people believed in him; they said, 'When the Christ appears, will he do more signs than this man has done?'

The opposition to Jesus is now becoming stronger (verse 1) and the tension between belief and unbelief greater. As people began to take sides or for against Jesus it is instructive to note the reasons men give for unbelief.

a. The brothers of Jesus—criticized His methods (verses 1–9)

It is clear that Jesus is working to a time-table—God's time-table. It is not yet the best time for Him to go publicly to Jerusalem (verse 6), so He remains quietly in Galilee. The Jewish Festival of Tabernacles lasted for eight days (end of September and beginning of October). Jesus arrived some time in the middle of the festivities, not at the start, as His brothers had suggested. His brothers cannot understand His reticence. They probably argued: 'Jesus has supernatural power. We have seen evidence of that. Why does He not work some spectacular miracle in Jerusalem, so that all may see without doubt that He is what He claims to be—God's Son and God's Messiah?' The only miracle attributed to Jesus in Jerusalem was the curing of the impotent man at the pool (John 5). You can almost hear the impatience and perhaps cynicism in their tone of voice when they say, 'If you do these things, show yourself to the world' (verse 4). Would not this prove to all that Jesus was no phoney? Why will He not demonstrate His power in the strategic city of Jerusalem? Jesus' brothers could not yet believe in Him. It could not have been easy for Jesus to be misunderstood by His own family.

Perhaps the brothers could not understand either why Jesus was so hated by the religious leaders of the day. Men prefer to support popular causes. Jesus seems to them to have thrown away His chances of being a popular success. Jesus' answer is revealing: '*The world . . . hates me because I testify of it that its works are evil*' (verse 7). None of us likes to be shown up by a good man.

We reject Jesus sometimes for the same reason as His brothers. We criticize His methods. We prefer not to talk about His death. We wonder why He led a minority movement, and why the church has always been like this. We sometimes blame the church in the same way. We accuse it for its lack of the spectacular, for its minority size. God's ways are not our ways. We must accept Jesus on His own terms or not at all. We must expect the church to be a minority movement, and sometimes a persecuted and hated minority, for, like Jesus, it lives in a world whose works are evil.

b. Many of the Jews in Jerusalem—criticized His character
(verses 10–31)

When Jesus eventually visited Jerusalem for the Jewish Feast of the Tabernacles, He discovered that there was a good deal of gossip about Him. Men were taking sides. No-one spoke openly because they were afraid of the reaction of officialdom. It is strange that even today in some church circles the mention of the name of Jesus in conversation can sometimes be followed by an embarrassing silence. Some could not avoid the conclusion that Jesus was a *good man* (verse 12). Those who criticized His character and took an opposite view could only make the following charges.

1. '*He is leading the people astray*' (verse 12). No-one defines in what way Jesus is doing this. No-one can give an example of any-one who has been led to corruption, or disloyalty to church or state. On one occasion Jesus said to His critics, 'Which of you convicts me of sin?' (John 8:46), and they could not answer one word. The sinlessness of Jesus, the blamelessness of His character, is one of the reasons for believing that He was divine.

2. '*He has a demon*' (verses 14–24). There were many in Jerusalem who were astonished at the authoritative teaching of Jesus, even though He had had no official theological and academic training in the schools of the Jewish Rabbis (verse 15). On another occasion the people had marvelled at His teaching because He spoke with authority, *and not as the scribes* (Matthew 7:28). Jesus explained that His teaching was authoritative because it was God's teaching. What God says, Jesus says; and anyone *willing to do God's will* would know this truth for certain. If we are willing to do God's will as He reveals it, we shall know that what Jesus says is God's truth (verse 17). Unfortunately, many of the Jews were not willing to do God's will. They had failed to obey the spirit of God's law (hence their criticism of Jesus for healing a man on the sabbath), they had judged Jesus superficially and falsely, and now they tried to blacken His character (verse 20) and to get rid of Him. It is a sign of weakness to abuse your opponent. Some-

times opposition to Christianity can too easily become like this.

The shallow thinking of the Jewish ecclesiastics is well shown up in this controversy about the sabbath and circumcision (verses 22–24). Circumcision, given to every male Jewish baby when eight days old as a sign of God's covenant or agreement with him and the family, involved a slight mutilation of the body. Jesus points out that if it is lawful to carry out an operation on the sabbath day which mutilates the flesh (circumcision), surely it cannot be unlawful to carry out an operation which makes the body whole (a healing miracle). Legalists often forget that people matter more than things, principles more than hard-and-fast rules.

3. *'We know where this man comes from'* (verses 25–32). Some of the people in Jerusalem began to accept the claims of Jesus, and wondered whether the authorities' delay in failing to forbid His teaching was a sign of their own conviction that He really was the Messiah (verses 25, 26).

Others thought they knew better, and doubted the honesty and integrity of Jesus' teaching. A little knowledge is sometimes a dangerous thing. They believed they knew the Scriptures better than Jesus. They dismissed His claims on the grounds that, whereas they all knew where Jesus came from, no-one would know where the Messiah would appear.*

Jesus, as ever (verse 28), affirms that the Jews do not know where Jesus comes from. For He comes from God, and they continually reveal the fact that they do not know God by their attitude to Himself. Yet again this stirs up the enemies of Jesus, but they cannot touch Him until God's time has come. Furthermore, many believed, as they weighed up the evidence, and considered the works of Jesus that so clearly authenticated His claims to be the Messiah.

It is right that we should consider carefully the methods, character, teaching and claims of Jesus Christ. This passage shows us the dangers of criticisms without reason, and accusation without evidence.

* The common belief was that the Messiah would *appear* suddenly, and no-one would know where He had come from. The Jews had a saying: 'Three things come wholly unexpectedly, the Messiah, a godsend, and a scorpion.'

17 THE CONFLICT CONTINUES

7:32–52

32 The Pharisees heard the crowd thus muttering about him, and the chief priests and Pharisees sent officers to arrest him. ³³Jesus then said, 'I shall be with you a little longer, and then I go to him who sent me; ³⁴you will seek me and you will not find me; where I am you cannot come.' ³⁵The Jews said to one another, 'Where does this man intend to go that we shall not find him? Does he intend to go to the Dispersion among the Greeks and teach the Greeks? ³⁶What does he mean by saying, "You will seek me and you will not find me," and, "Where I am you cannot come"?'

37 On the last day of the feast, the great day, Jesus stood up and proclaimed, 'If any one thirst, let him come to me and drink. ³⁸He who believes in me, as the scripture has said, "Out of his heart shall flow rivers of living water." ³⁹Now this he said about the Spirit, which those who believed in him were to receive; for as yet the Spirit had not been given, because Jesus was not yet glorified.

40 When they heard these words, some of the people said, 'This is really the prophet.' ⁴¹Others said, 'This is the Christ.' But some said, 'Is the Christ to come from Galilee? ⁴²Has not the scripture said that the Christ is descended from David, and comes from Bethlehem, the village where David was?' ⁴³So there was a division among the people over him. ⁴⁴Some of them wanted to arrest him, but no one laid hands on him.

45 The officers then went back to the chief priests and Pharisees, who said to them, 'Why did you not bring him?' ⁴⁶The officers answered, 'No man ever spoke like this man!' ⁴⁷The Pharisees answered them, 'Are you led astray, you also? ⁴⁸Have any of the authorities or of the Pharisees believed in him? ⁴⁹But this crowd, who do not know the law, are accursed.' ⁵⁰Nicodemus, who had gone to him before, and who was one of them, said to them, ⁵¹'Does our law judge a man without first giving him a hearing and learning what he does?' ⁵²They replied, 'Are you from Galilee too? Search and you will see that no prophet is to rise from Galilee.'

John now describes the leaders of the opposition, the Pharisees. They were the separatists or Puritans of Judaism. Their name is derived from the verb *parash*, 'to separate'; and their aim was to withdraw from all evil associations and to obey in detail every precept of the oral and written law.*

Many Pharisees became excessively self-righteous; others, like Nicodemus (see chapter 3 and 7:50), set a high moral and spiritual standard. It is interesting to remember that of all the sects of Judaism, Pharisaism has alone survived. It has become the modern orthodox Judaism of today which follows a Pharisaic pattern of morality, ceremonialism and legalism.

The *chief priests* at this time were almost certainly Sadducees. The *Sadducees* was the title of the priestly party in the time of Christ. They were a political party and collaborators with their Roman masters. They differed from the Pharisees in many of their beliefs, as they acknowledged as authoritative only the first five books of the Bible, and they denied the supernatural—especially the existence of angels and spirits (Acts 23:8) and the resurrection after death. They did not want a Messiah, as this would interfere with their own vested interests under the Romans.

There is no doubt that the teaching of Jesus was a threat to the privilege and position of the Sadducees and many of the Pharisees. Some of the hardest things that Jesus said were said in rebuke of the hypocrisy and self-righteousness of these religious leaders (see Matthew 23). Furthermore, some of these ecclesiastics no doubt believed that it was important to keep on the right side of the Roman authorities. Palestine was an occupied country, and if the followers of Jesus started an unwise uprising, they would bring trouble down on the Pharisees themselves. Again, Jesus had claimed to be God. There was no question of examining whether or not Jesus had a right to such a claim. In their eyes it was blasphemy. That was sufficient.

So at last, hearing of the constant mutterings of the crowds in Jerusalem, the chief priests and Pharisees sent officers to arrest Jesus. I think we must imagine that Jesus is speaking to the Temple police, with the scribes and the Pharisees and the rest of the people

* For an interesting list of seven types of Pharisees, see Merrill C. Tenney, *New Testament Survey*, p. 110.

standing around and listening intently. In the dialogue that follows the arrival of the police, we cannot fail to notice certain points concerning Jesus.

a. His complete control of the situation (verses 32-36)

Jesus is completely unafraid of the threats of men, and shows that He is quietly and voluntarily moving towards the end of His earthly ministry, when He will return to His heavenly Father (verse 33). The Jews show how little they have listened to His teaching or understood it. Yet Jesus implies that their rejection of it will one day exclude them from the presence of God. 'I go to him who sent me . . . *where I am you cannot come*' (verses 34-36). Man cannot do whatever he likes with Jesus. Nor can man choose his own time. It is Jesus Christ who is in control of circumstances, and life and death itself. It is possible to reject Jesus Christ so often that we no longer *want* to listen to Him.

b. His simple offer of life (verses 37-39)

These words were spoken on the last (eighth) day of the Festival of Tabernacles. This feast was compulsory for all adult male Jews who lived within twenty miles of Jerusalem. The purpose of the feast was to remind the Jews of their wanderings in the wilderness before they reached the promised land: 'that your generations may know that I made the people of Israel dwell in booths when I brought them out of the land of Egypt' (Leviticus 23:40-43). The festival was also a harvest thanksgiving, sometimes called 'the Feast of the Ingathering' (Exodus 23:16) to be celebrated 'at the end of the year'. Indeed, it included thanksgiving for all God's gifts. Josephus called it 'the holiest and the greatest Festival among the Jews'.*

It was on this last day of the feast that Jesus directed the thoughts of all the worshippers once again to Himself. He turned their thoughts away from the water that refreshed their bodies to that water which refreshes the soul. Jesus could provide refreshment of spirit which would not only bubble up inside a man but overflow

* Josephus, *Antiquities of the Jews*, iii. 10. 4.

78

to the refreshment of others. He suggests that as we cannot live, physically, without water, so we cannot live, spiritually, without Christ. Men would find this true if only they would come to Him and receive the 'life' He was offering them. Once more Jesus insists that He is offering a new inner quality of life and satisfaction which must be received by faith. John adds the comment (verse 39) that the truth of these words was experienced after the death, resurrection and ascension of Jesus, when the disciples received the gift of God's Holy Spirit (see also John 14:16).

c. His challenge to faith (verses 40–52)

Once again a simple and personal challenge to come to Him creates a division among the people. There were many different reactions to Jesus Christ then, as there are today.

1. *Some believed that Jesus was 'the prophet'* (verse 40). Yet a prophet's authority is derived. A prophet says 'thus says the Lord'. Surely Jesus is more than a prophet. He says, 'Of a truth *I* say unto you . . .' He says, 'Come to *me* . . . learn from *me*' (Matthew 11:28, 29).

2. *Some believed that He was 'the Christ'* (verse 41). At least, they gave intellectual assent to this claim. But Christian belief involves more than intellectual assent (see John 6).

3. *Some were agnostic,* for they did not know sufficient about Him to make a decision (verse 42). Quite rightly they searched the Scriptures to check His claims. They had not discovered that Jesus was indeed descended from David and born at Bethlehem. Or were they keeping Jesus at arm's length by engaging in a theological argument for its own sake?

4. *Some were antagonistic,* possibly out of jealousy, or fear, or guilty conscience, or unwillingness to change their lives, and they wanted to remove the challenge of Jesus' life and teaching by getting Him out of the way (verse 44). Like the man mentioned in the Psalms, they hated Him 'without cause' (Psalm 35:19).

5. *Some were interested.* The Temple police, for example, are intrigued, impressed and almost believing. 'No man ever spoke like this man!' (verse 46). They go out to silence the man. They come back amazed and deeply moved. The only answer the Pharisees

can give them is: 'This is not the official teaching of the church. None of the church leaders believes in Him.' This presupposes of course that only the scholars and ecclesiastics can understand the truths of God, an impression that some church pronouncements of our own day do little to avoid. This was religious, intellectual and social snobbery of the worst kind. It is still true today that some reject Jesus for the same reasons. They think themselves too clever or too respectable to become enthusiasts for Jesus Christ. They stop at religion without Christ. They are religious but not Christian.*

6. *Some wanted more time to think.* Like Nicodemus, they wanted more time to weigh up the evidence. In a typically cautious and scholarly way he asks the question of the other members of the Jewish Cabinet, or Sanhedrin, 'Does our law judge a man without first giving him a hearing and learning what he does?' (verse 51). For Nicodemus, it was not only a question of justice, it was also a concern for truth. The suggestion that Nicodemus spoke for justice only because of some supposed local Galilaean loyalty shows how desperate these men were for arguments. If they had bothered to ask a few more questions, and had really wanted to know the truth, they would have soon discovered that Jesus had not been born in Galilee anyway (verse 52). Nicodemus was slow, and still sitting on the fence, but his basic attitude was honest and good. The pressure of circumstances and honest seeking were one day to lead him to open and unashamed allegiance to Jesus (see John 19).

* The word 'Christian' was first a nickname, probably a word of abuse, given to the early followers of Jesus Christ, because of their enthusiasm and whole-heartedness in following Him in the face of persecution and death (Acts 11:26).

18 JESUS' ATTITUDE TO IMMORALITY
7:53 – 8:11

53 **They went each to his own house, ¹but Jesus went to the Mount of Olives. ²Early in the morning he came again to the temple; all the people came to him, and he sat down and taught them. ³The scribes and the Pharisees brought a woman who had been caught in adultery, and placing her in the midst ⁴they said to him, 'Teacher, this woman has been caught in the act of adultery. ⁵Now in the law Moses commanded us to stone such. What do you say about her?' ⁶This they said to test him, that they might have some charge to bring against him. Jesus bent down and wrote with his finger on the ground. ⁷And as they continued to ask him, he stood up and said to them, 'Let him who is without sin among you be the first to throw a stone at her.' ⁸And once more he bent down and wrote with his finger on the ground. ⁹But when they heard it, they went away, one by one, beginning with the eldest, and Jesus was left alone with the woman standing before him. ¹⁰Jesus looked up and said to her, 'Woman, where are they? Has no one condemned you?' ¹¹She said, 'No one, Lord.' And Jesus said, 'Neither do I condemn you; go, and do not sin again.'**

Some manuscripts place this moving incident at the end of John's Gospel or after Luke 21:38. We are not concerned in this commentary to go into the details of textual criticism. It is sufficient to say that there is little reason to doubt the authenticity of this story, whether or not this is the best chronological position for it.

In the time of Jesus, difficult legal and moral questions were taken to a Rabbi for a decision. Hence the seemingly polite request of the scribes and Pharisees, 'Teacher, this woman has been caught in the act of adultery. Now the law of Moses commanded us to stone such. What do you say about her?' The action of these men was, of course, an appalling one, especially as they realized that whatever answer Jesus gave they could turn it against Him (verse 6). The law of Moses laid down that 'if a man commits adultery with the wife of his neighbour, both the adulterer and the adultress shall be put to death' (Leviticus 20:10). In Deuteronomy 22:13–24 it is determined that death shall be by stoning. So if Jesus pardoned the woman, the scribes and Pharisees would condemn Jesus for disregarding the law of Moses. If Jesus said she ought to be stoned, He would not only be accused of being unmerciful and harsh, but He would probably come up against the Roman authorities as well, for the Jews had no power to pass or carry out the death sentence on anyone.

Before Jesus answers, He bends down and writes with His finger on the ground. Whether He did this to gain time before He answered such a vile question, or because He was overcome with a terrible sense of shame, so that He could not look upon a scene that showed up so clearly the hypocrisy and cruelty of the Pharisees, we do not know. Some commentators suggest that He was writing in the dust the sins of the very men who were accusing the woman. The normal Greek word for 'to write' is *graphein*: here the word is *katagraphein* which can mean 'to write down a record against someone'. Whatever the reason for this strange action, the men continued to press their question avidly upon him.

The answer that Jesus gives not only turns the tables on His critics, but lays down principles that help us to discover a right attitude to immorality in our own day.

a. We are all sinners

Many people today define sin in terms of the kind of things we read about in the newspapers—rape, adultery, murder, crime, and so on. The scribes and Pharisees of Jesus' day were inclined to think in a similar way. To sin was to break the law. But even someone deliberately hunting out and persecuting Christians, like Saul of Tarsus, could claim that 'as touching the law' he was 'blameless', for to him keeping the law was just a matter of avoiding certain sins such as adultery, murder and stealing.

Jesus defined sin more clearly. Sin was indeed 'breaking God's law', but man could do this by loving money more than God, by nourishing the lustful thought as well as committing the act of adultery, by hating a man as well as killing him, by failing to do positive good as well as avoiding evil. Indeed, according to Jesus

82

Christ, we sin and break the greatest commandment of all when we fail to love God with all our heart, mind, soul and strength and our neighbour as ourself (see Matthew 5:21, 22, 27, 28; 22:37-40). No wonder Saul of Tarsus could write, after he had become a Christian and understood the perfect standard of God's law, 'For there is no distinction; since all have sinned and fall short of the glory of God' (Romans 3:23).

Sin is defined in the New Testament as 'missing the mark' and 'breaking the law', and if we offend in one point only we are still guilty (see James 2:10). It is not only the Pharisees who are rebuked at the convicting words of Jesus, 'Let him who is *without sin* among you be the first to throw a stone at her' (verse 7). When they heard it they slunk away (verse 9). If we understand 'sin' as breaking God's standards in thought, as well as word and deed, we too shall be ashamed before the purity and sinlessness of Jesus Christ.

b. Sin is always condemned

'Jesus was left alone with the woman standing before him.' No doubt her eyes were on the ground, her clothes dishevelled, her face a mixture of sullenness, shame and hope. 'Has no one condemned you?' She said, 'No one, Lord.' And Jesus said, 'Neither do I condemn you; go, and do not sin again.'

What is clear in this story is that Jesus does not condemn her act of adultery more than the Pharisees' act of cruelty and hypocrisy. In Jesus' eyes we may well believe that adultery is no better or worse than hypocrisy. Both the woman and her accusers have *sinned*. They have broken God's law. They deserve God's judgment. 'Go, and do not *sin* again.' Sin matters to Jesus. It mattered so much to Jesus that He was prepared to die on a cross to bear its judgment and its shame.

Those writers who argue that Jesus displaced law by love have failed to notice that Jesus does not hesitate to call the woman's act of adultery *sin*. For Jesus, love would be blind without the law to guide it. 'If you love me,' said Jesus on another occasion, '*you will keep my commandments*' (John 14:15).

83

c. Jesus is altogether merciful

Jesus condemns sin, but loves the sinner. If we slink away from Jesus like the Pharisees we may never receive His mercy and forgiveness. The woman stayed in the presence of Jesus and heard His words of mercy and hope, 'Neither do I condemn you; go, and do not sin again.' There is no-one outside the love and mercy of Jesus.

In Camus' novel, *The Fall*, Jean-Baptiste Clemence, a once successful Paris barrister who had fallen into debauchery and immorality, becomes terribly aware of his own guilt, and believes that religion can no longer help him. 'I am inclined to see religion . . . as a huge laundering venture—as it was once, but briefly, for exactly three years, and it wasn't called religion. Since then soap has been lacking, our faces are dirty, and we wipe one another's nose.'* It is true that religion cannot make us clean from sin. But Jesus can. What Camus failed to realize was that Jesus is alive today to offer complete forgiveness and mercy to those who come to Him. He does not condone sin. He went to the cross to bear its consequences. But because of His death for sin He offers to those who turn from their sin and trust in Him complete forgiveness and the prospect of a new life—'Go, and do not sin again.'

19 JESUS, THE LIGHT OF THE WORLD
8:12–30

12 Again Jesus spoke to them, saying, 'I am the light of the world; he who follows me will not walk in darkness, but will have the light of life.' 13The Pharisees then said to him, 'You are bearing witness to yourself; your testimony is not true.' 14Jesus answered, 'Even if I do bear witness to myself, my testimony is true, for I know whence I have come and whither

* Albert Camus, *The Fall*, p. 82.

I am going, but you do not know whence I come or whither I am going, ¹⁵You judge according to the flesh, I judge no one. ¹⁶Yet even if I do judge, my judgment is true, for it is not I alone that judge, but I and he who sent me. ¹⁷In your law it is written that the testimony of two men is true; ¹⁸I bear witness to myself, and the Father who sent me bears witness to me.' ¹⁹They said to him therefore, 'Where is your Father?' Jesus answered, 'You know neither me nor my Father; if you knew me, you would know my Father also.' ²⁰These words he spoke in the treasury, as he taught in the temple; but no one arrested him, because his hour had not yet come.

21 Again he said to them, 'I go away, and you will seek me and die in your sin; where I am going, you cannot come.' ²²Then said the Jews, 'Will he kill himself, since he says, "Where I am going, you cannot come"?' ²³He said to them, 'You are from below, I am from above; you are of this world, I am not of this world. ²⁴I told you that you would die in your sins, for you will die in your sins unless you believe that I am he.' ²⁵They said to him, 'Who are you?' Jesus said to them, 'Even what I have told you from the beginning. ²⁶I have much to say about you and much to judge; but he who sent me is true, and I declare to the world what I have heard from him.' ²⁷They did not understand that he spoke to them of the Father. ²⁸So Jesus said, 'When you have lifted up the Son of man, then you will know that I am he, and that I do nothing on my own authority but speak thus as the Father taught me. ²⁹And he who sent me is with me; he has not left me alone, for I always do what is pleasing to him.' ³⁰As he spoke thus, many believed in him.

If the writers and dramatists of today reflect the attitude of the majority of ordinary people, then most of us are aware of the darkness and uncertainty of living in the twentieth century. In Samuel Beckett's play, *Waiting for Godot*, the main characters are two tramps who in utter boredom wait for Godot to turn up. They don't know who Godot is, and at the end of the play, when he has failed to appear, one tramp says to the other, 'Well, shall we go?' The reply comes, 'Yes, let's go.' But the final stage direction says simply 'they do not move'. There have been many interpretations of this play, but there is little doubt that it reflects the twentieth-century mood. We are waiting for something, maybe for someone, to turn up. Some light to shine in the darkness.

So were the Jews in the days of Jesus. At this same Feast of

Tabernacles (see John 7) a ceremony had begun called 'the illumination of the Temple'. Hundreds of Jews were gathered in the Temple waiting for God's help and guidance in their lives, knowing the darkness of ignorance and moral failure. Their hope lay in a Messiah who would come as a light in the darkness. As dusk began to fall upon the Temple courtyard, the four great golden candelabra were lit, and sent out a blaze of light which flooded every courtyard, and, as some said, shone all over Jerusalem. Some pious Jews began to dance and to sing Hebrew chants. 'The Lord is my light,' they cried. 'By His light I walked through darkness.'

It was on this day that some of the crowd heard Jesus say, 'I am the light of the world; he who follows me will not walk in darkness, but will have the light of life.' Was Jesus the Messiah, they asked? Was He claiming to be God who alone is 'the Light'? The Pharisees of course again accused Him of lying. They tried to support their contention by quoting the Jewish law, that if a statement was to be regarded as true, it must be supported by at least two witnesses. For example, in the book of Deuteronomy we read, 'On the evidence of two witnesses or of three witnesses he that is to die shall be put to death' (Deuteronomy 17:6). When it was convenient to them, of course, they quietly forgot this law (see John 18:19–24).

Jesus answers their point by claiming that His own unique relationship to God dispenses with the necessity for any further witness to Himself (verse 14); but in fact if they knew God themselves they would have seen that God the Father had also witnessed to the truth of Jesus' claims (verse 18). The answer Jesus gives enables us to consider again some of His claims.

a. Jesus claimed a unique relationship with God

No ordinary man could have made the claims that Jesus made about Himself without being deluded, or suffering megalomania. We have only to imagine a popular preacher today standing up and saying some of these things to realize how astonishing these claims are. The words of verse 14 might sound ambiguous to some of the crowd; but they seem to mean that Jesus knew His future destiny as clearly as His pre-existent state. As He said later on (verse 23), 'You are from below, I am from above; you are of this world, I am not of this world.' Jesus did not begin to exist when He was born as a baby at Bethlehem. He claims that He existed before that, and that He came from the presence of God (verses 23, 26). Because of this unique relationship with God always, He claims the authority to judge with the same perfect judgment as God (verses 15, 16).

Furthermore, if His opponents really knew God they would know Him also. Jesus' relationship with His Father was so close that He could imply that to know Him was to know God, and to listen to Him was to listen to God (verses 26–28). Strangely enough, Jesus predicts that the Jews would not recognize Him as divine* until they had lifted Him up on a cross to die (verse 28). The almighty God was to reveal Himself most clearly to men when His Son Jesus Christ was crucified in weakness.

b. Jesus claimed to be perfect like God (verse 29)

'For I always do what is pleasing to him.' Many great saints have been able to say 'God is with me; he has not left me alone' (verse 29); but no good man would say 'I *always* do what is pleasing to him' unless he was perfect; and God alone is absolutely pure and absolutely good. Down the ages the greatest saints have always been those who have been humbly aware of their failings and short-comings. Paul, towards the end of his life, found it appropriate to call himself 'the foremost of sinners' (see 1 Timothy 1:15). One of the well known Christian hymns expresses it in the words:

> 'And they who fain would serve Thee best
> Are conscious most of wrong within.'

The nearer we get to the light of God's purity, the darker our own lives are seen to be.

Yet Jesus, here and elsewhere, assumes this purity and sinless-ness of character. He never apologizes or confesses sin. He says to His enemies on another occasion, 'Which of you convicts me of sin?' (John 8:46) and no-one answers. Furthermore, His closest friends, in spite of their honesty about one another's failures, speak

---

*'I am he' was the same word in Hebrew as one of the divine names of God which the Jew never spoke out of reverence for God. Jesus may well be deliberately using it here as a claim to be God.

of Jesus as one who was like a lamb 'without blemish or spot' (1 Peter 1:19) and one who 'committed no sin; no guile was found on his lips' (1 Peter 2:22). 'In him', said John the apostle, 'there is no sin' (1 John 3:5). Even today when men criticize the church, and the clergy, and other Christians, they very rarely criticize Jesus Christ. He is the one perfectly good and sinless man. But as Jesus Himself once said to a young man who was seeking the truth, 'No one is good but God alone' (Mark 10:18).

Was Jesus then deluded or divine?

A megalomaniac can make extravagant claims. But as C. S. Lewis once wrote: 'The discrepancy between the depth and sanity, and (let me add) shrewdness of His moral teaching, and the rampant megalomania which must lie behind His theological teaching unless He is indeed God, has never been satisfactorily got over.'* Furthermore, those who talk 'big' usually act 'big'. Hitler made great claims for himself and acted arrogantly and brutally. Jesus uttered self-centred claims, but acted selflessly and sacrificially. Is selflessness and love a characteristic of God or of a madman? If we believe that Jesus is divine, God become man, then the tension between His self-centred claims and His selfless life is resolved. For if He is God, He has a right to make such claims, and at the same time He will act with selflessness and love.

It would have been remarkable, if not impossible, for many to have believed in Jesus after He had spoken these words (verse 30) unless His life had backed up His words. But with Jesus His life endorsed His claims.

* C. S. Lewis, *Miracles.*

20 THE MARKS OF A GENUINE DISCIPLE
8:31-59

31 Jesus then said to the Jews who had believed in him, 'If you continue in my word, you are truly my disciples, 32and you will know the truth, and the truth will make you free.' 33They answered him, 'We are descendants of Abraham, and have never been in bondage to anyone. How is it that you say, "You will be made free"?'

34 Jesus answered them, 'Truly, truly, I say to you, every one who commits sin is a slave to sin. 35The slave does not continue in the house for ever; the son continues for ever. 36So if the Son makes you free, you will be free indeed. 37I know that you are descendants of Abraham; yet you seek to kill me, because my word finds no place in you. 38I speak of what I have seen with my Father, and you do what you have heard from your father.'

39 They answered him, 'Abraham is our father.' Jesus said to them, 'If you were Abraham's children, you would do what Abraham did, 40but now you seek to kill me, a man who has told you the truth which I heard from God; this is not what Abraham did. 41You do what your father did.' They said to him, 'We were not born of fornication; we have one Father, even God.' 42Jesus said to them, 'If God were your Father, you would love me, for I proceeded and came forth from God; I came not of my own accord, but he sent me. 43Why do you not understand what I say? It is because you cannot bear to hear my word. 44You are of your father the devil, and your will is to do your father's desires. He was a murderer from the beginning, and has nothing to do with the truth, because there is no truth in him. When he lies, he speaks according to his own nature, for he is a liar and the father of lies. 45But, because I tell the truth, you do not believe me. 46Which of you convicts me of sin? If I tell the truth, why do you not believe me? 47He who is of God hears the words of God; the reason why you do not hear them is that you are not of God.'

48 The Jews answered him, 'Are we not right in saying that you are a Samaritan and have a demon?' 49Jesus answered, 'I have not a demon; I honour my Father, and you dishonour me. 50Yet I do not seek my own glory; there is One who seeks

it and he will be the judge. ⁵¹Truly, truly, I say to you, if any one keeps my word, he will never see death.' ⁵²The Jews said to him, 'Now we know that you have a demon. Abraham died, as did the prophets; and you say, "If any one keeps my word, he will never taste death." ⁵³Are you greater than our father Abraham, who died? And the prophets died! Whom do you make yourself to be?' ⁵⁴Jesus answered, 'If I glorify myself, my glory is nothing; it is my Father who glorifies me, of whom you say that he is your God. ⁵⁵But you have not known him; I know him. If I said, I do not know him, I should be a liar like you; but I do know him and I keep his word. ⁵⁶Your father Abraham rejoiced that he was to see my day; he saw it and was glad.' ⁵⁷The Jews then said to him, 'You are not yet fifty years old, and have you seen Abraham?' ⁵⁸Jesus said to them, 'Truly, truly, I say to you, before Abraham was, I am.' ⁵⁹So they took up stones to throw at him; but Jesus hid himself, and went out of the temple.

It is easy enough to be moved by an appealing sermon or a convincing piece of logic, and to say, 'Oh yes, I believe in Jesus.' We are not sure how genuine the belief of these Jews really was: but as Jesus turns to speak to them (verse 31), He teaches us some of the marks of a genuine disciple.

a. A genuine disciple continues and does not give up (verses 31–33)

'If you continue in my word, you are truly my disciples.' Jesus said on another occasion, 'he who endures to the end will be saved' (Mark 13:13). It is possible to *say* we believe and to make some 'decision' for Christ. But the only sure evidence for the genuineness of our faith is that we are still obeying the words of Jesus Christ, knowing the truth and enjoying its freedom.

b. A genuine disciple enjoys freedom and not slavery (verses 34–38)

Real freedom is not to be found in resisting the claims of Jesus Christ, or in trusting in religious privileges. Religion does not make us free, for it cannot free us from sinful habits and self-centred thinking. 'Every one who commits sin is a slave to sin.' It is easy to see how this is true for a drunkard, or a sex pervert, or a drug addict. But it is also true of the person who is a slave to men's opinions, or the world's fashions, or that thing 'which everyone does', or 'keeping up with the Jones's'. Even religious people can become slaves to ecclesiastical practices or jargon, or prejudices or conventions. Jesus promises to set us free if we continue to obey His word and know the truth in Him. For it is the truth that sets us free.

c. A genuine disciple behaves like a child of God, not a child of the devil (verses 39–47)

The Jews claimed to be the children of Abraham, and they were such by physical descent; but they were certainly not the children of God, or they would not be seeking to kill Jesus. Nor would a child of God make suggestive remarks about the illegitimacy of Jesus' birth (verse 41). These men, suggests Jesus, have never become God's children, because they clearly do not exhibit God's nature. They have not the hallmark of love. They do not love Jesus although He has 'come forth from God' (verse 42). If they were God's children they would understand the teaching of Jesus, instead of hating to hear it (verse 43). They would tell the truth instead of lies. They would acknowledge the truth instead of denying it. For although they can find no fault in Jesus (verse 46), yet they are prepared to slander Him (verse 48). These men have a family likeness to the father of lies, the devil, rather than God the heavenly Father. 'He who is of God hears the words of God; the reason why you do not hear them is that you are not of God.'

d. A genuine disciple honours Jesus Christ and does not dishonour Him (verses 48–59)

'You dishonour me,' Jesus said. In spite of their religious professions these men were prepared to insult Jesus (verse 48), to reject His claims (verse 52) and to put Him to death (verse 59). Jesus patiently continues to reiterate His own claims and motives. He seeks only to honour God (verses 49, 50). His words are a matter of life and death: 'If any one keeps my word, he will never see death' (verses 51, 52). He obeys God and God honours Him—to say anything else would be a lie. Even Abraham longed for the day when Jesus would come to this earth, for, said Jesus, 'before Abraham was, I am'. This is perhaps the clearest direct claim to be God that Jesus uttered. He makes it with great emphasis ('Truly, truly'). He includes the thought of His own previous existence before He was born on earth. But there is no mistaking His claim to be God when He takes upon His own lips the title 'I am'. Hundreds of years before, according to the Old Testament, God had spoken to Moses and said, 'Say this to the people of Israel, "I AM has sent me unto you."' (Exodus 3:14). This title 'I AM' speaks of God's eternal, timeless existence. Jesus had used this phrase before in the same discussion (verses 24, 28). We know that the Jews clearly believed He was claiming to be God, for they took up stones to stone Him. The Jewish penalty for blasphemy was death by stoning. Jesus escaped from the angry mob, but knew that the issues of belief and unbelief were becoming clearer.

The genuine disciple is glad to honour Jesus as God. He can say, as Thomas did later, 'My Lord and my God!' (John 20:28).

21 THE PROBLEM OF SUFFERING
9:1–12

1 As he passed by, he saw a man blind from his birth. ²And his disciples asked him, 'Rabbi, who sinned, this man or his parents, that he was born blind?' ³Jesus answered, 'It was not that this man sinned, or his parents, but that the works of God might be made manifest in him. ⁴We must work the works of him who sent me, while it is day; night comes, when no one can work. ⁵As long as I am in the world, I am the light of the world.' ⁶As he said this, he spat on the ground and made clay of the spittle and anointed the man's eyes with the clay, ⁷saying to him, 'Go, wash in the pool of Siloam' (which means

Sent). So he went and washed and came back seeing. ⁸The neighbours and those who had seen him before as a beggar, said, 'Is not this the man who used to sit and beg?' ⁹Some said, 'It is he'; others said, 'No, but he is like him.' He said, 'I am the man.' ¹⁰They said to him, 'Then how were your eyes opened?' ¹¹He answered, 'The man called Jesus made clay and anointed my eyes and said to me, "Go to Siloam and wash"; so I went and washed and received my sight.' ¹²They said to him, 'Where is he?' He said, 'I do not know.'

When Jesus gave sight to a scruffy blind beggar sitting in rags at the side of a dusty road, He once again made a healing miracle the sign of a profound spiritual truth. 'As long as I am in the world,' said Jesus, 'I am the light of the world' (verse 5). But before we consider the significance of these words, this incident has something to say about one very common barrier to belief: *the problem of suffering.*

The disciples were worried by this problem. Knowing that the beggar had been blind from birth they said, 'Rabbi, who sinned, this man or his parents, that he was born blind?' The disciples assumed that suffering was the result of sin. In one sense they were right. According to the Bible, when God made the world in the beginning it was perfect or, in the words recorded in Genesis, it was 'very good'. There was 'in the beginning' no sin, no suffering, no disease, no pain. Man enjoyed perfect friendship with God. But God had not made man an automaton, but a person who was able to exercise choice. As a result of man's disobedience and rebellion against God's will, that is, his 'Fall', man's original innocence was lost (see Genesis 3). Sin, suffering, disease and disorder entered into God's world. This is the Bible's explanation of man's basic self-centredness. Because of the unity of the human race, all men have fallen and disobeyed 'in Adam', and man has inherited a selfish, sinful nature. This is the cause of much suffering today. As the apostle James wrote: 'What causes wars, and what causes fightings among you? Is it not your passions that are at war in your members? You desire and do not have; so you kill. And you covet and cannot obtain; so you fight and wage war' (James 4:1, 2).

Man's sinful human nature, and the reality of evil in the world, go a long way to help us to understand the cause of human suffering. The humanist's philosophy of the essential goodness of human nature is hopelessly unrealistic in comparison and many modern writers have now discarded it. The novelist, William Golding, for example, expresses the purpose of his novels as trying 'to trace the defects of society back to the defects of human nature'.* The French novelist, Camus, who was very concerned about the whole problem of human suffering and rejected the Christian explanation, was not so foolish as to imagine that man is innocent. In the words of Jean-Baptiste Clemence in *The Fall* he believed that 'we cannot assert the innocence of anyone, whereas we can state with certainty the guilt of all'.†

In general, then, all human suffering is the consequence of the Fall (see Genesis 3:16–19). God is not the author of suffering. In many particular instances suffering is caused by man's inhumanity to man. But still there is the question raised by this story, why is a man *born* blind? Is it the direct result of his own sin or the sin of his parents? Jesus does more than give a straight answer to this one question. He throws some shafts of light upon the whole problem of suffering. The light Jesus gives is enough to help us to face up to human suffering, even though we may not fully understand it or escape it in this life.

a. Suffering is not always a direct result of sin

Some of the Rabbis believed that suffering was always the direct result of sin. It is difficult for us to understand how a man *born* blind could be responsible for this blindness. But some of the Jewish theologians had the strange idea that a baby could begin to sin while he was still in his mother's womb, or even in a pre-existent state before he was conceived. The other possibility was that this man's blindness was due to his parents' sin. This is sometimes possible. Recently we have read of babies who have been born with all the symptoms of drug-addiction, because their mothers were addicts. None of us lives to himself. But in this case Jesus makes it quite clear that suffering is not always the direct result of a man's own sin or the sin of his parents. Some of the greatest saints have been some of the greatest sufferers.

* Quoted in Stuart Babbage, *The Mark of Cain*, p. 25.
† Albert Camus, *The Fall*, p. 81.

b. Suffering is not part of the direct will of God

'It's God's will, I suppose,' mutters a heroic sufferer. The Bible makes clear that sin and suffering is not part of God's direct will for the world. But it can be part of His permissive will. God allowed this blind man to suffer for a purpose; 'It was not that this man sinned, or his parents, but that the works of God might be made manifest in him' (verse 3). So this man's suffering was overruled by God *for his benefit*. Through his blindness and need he had an encounter with Jesus Christ which changed his life. A man once said to me, 'I thank God for polio.' I knew what he meant. It was not that polio is good, or God's will for His world. But for this man, this illness which afflicted two members of his family was the means of leading him to a personal faith in Jesus Christ.

Again, suffering can be *for God's glory*. The sufferings of Jesus are the supreme example. In this story too other men learnt of God's plan for their spiritual sight and healing through the healing of this blind man, and so God was glorified. I once visited a seriously ill girl in hospital whose courage and gaiety and Christian witness made a profound impression upon the hospital staff. God was honoured by her courageous suffering. God strengthened her in it. God may sometimes allow suffering for man's good and for His own glory. We can realize this when we remember that many virtues such as patience, courage, humility, pity and compassion grow most strongly in the garden of suffering. We could add to this the fact that pain is a necessary protection for man against injury, and essential to man's physical survival.

c. Suffering is not inconsistent with the love of God

Jesus is the light of the world. He came to men in the darkness of suffering and sin to bring healing to their bodies as well as illumination to their minds. He showed that He loves men by many acts of healing and compassion. And we know that He calls us to relieve suffering where we find it. In this story He moves quickly from theological discussion to active love—much more quickly than we do! (verses 3–6). He tests the man's faith and obedience. It is the man's faith and obedience which are the conditions of healing. The blind man sees (verse 7).

If God is revealed in Jesus in the way that the writer asserts (see John 1), then in this story we have further evidence of God's love and concern for human sufferers. Further evidence may be seen in the sufferings of Jesus Himself (see John 19). Furthermore, the Christian believes that by the death and resurrection of Jesus Christ, sin and evil were defeated, and the gateway to heaven opened. In heaven, according to the author of the book of Revelation, followers of Jesus Christ can look forward to this experience: God 'will wipe away every tear from their eyes, and death shall be no more, neither shall there be mourning nor crying nor pain any more, for the former things have passed away' (Revelation 21:4). Then God's perfect will shall be done, and all suffering banished.*

22 THE PROBLEM OF SPIRITUAL BLINDNESS
9:13–41

13 They brought to the Pharisees the man who had formerly been blind. ¹⁴Now it was a sabbath day when Jesus made the clay and opened his eyes. ¹⁵The Pharisees again asked him how he had received his sight. And he said to them, 'He put clay on my eyes, and I washed, and I see.' ¹⁶Some of the Pharisees said, 'This man is not from God, for he does not keep the sabbath.' But others said, 'How can a man who is a sinner do such signs?' There was a division among them. ¹⁷So they again said to the blind man, 'What do you say about him, since he has opened your eyes?' He said, 'He is a prophet.'
18 The Jews did not believe that he had been blind and had received his sight, until they called the parents of the man who had received his sight, ¹⁹and asked them, 'Is this your son, who you say was born blind? How then does he now see?' ²⁰His parents answered, 'We know that this is our son, and that he was born blind; ²¹but how he now sees we do not know, nor do we know who opened his eyes. Ask him; he is of age, he will speak for himself.' ²²His parents said this because they

* For further reading on this subject see C. S. Lewis, *The Problem of Pain.*

feared the Jews, for the Jews had already agreed that if any one should confess him to be Christ, he was to be put out of the synagogue. ²³Therefore his parents said, 'He is of age, ask him.'

24 So for the second time they called the man who had been blind, and said to him, 'Give God the praise; we know that this man is a sinner.' ²⁵He answered, 'Whether he is a sinner, I do not know; one thing I know, that though I was blind, now I see.' ²⁶They said to him, 'What did he do to you? How did he open your eyes?' ²⁷He answered them, 'I have told you already, and you would not listen. Why do you want to hear it again? Do you too want to become his disciples?' ²⁸And they reviled him, saying, 'You are his disciple, but we are disciples of Moses. ²⁹We know that God has spoken to Moses, but as for this man, we do not know where he comes from.' ³⁰The man answered, 'Why, this is a marvel! You do not know where he comes from, and yet he opened my eyes. ³¹We know that God does not listen to sinners, but if any one is a worshipper of God and does his will, God listens to him. ³²Never since the world began has it been heard that any one opened the eyes of a man born blind. ³³If this man were not from God, he could do nothing.' ³⁴They answered him, 'You were born in utter sin, and would you teach us?' And they cast him out.

35 Jesus heard that they had cast him out, and having found him he said, 'Do you believe in the Son of man?' ³⁶He answered, 'And who is he, sir, that I may believe in him?' ³⁷Jesus said to him, 'You have seen him, and it is he who speaks to you.' ³⁸He said, 'Lord, I believe'; and he worshipped him. ³⁹Jesus said, 'For judgment I came into this world, that those who do not see may see, and that those who see may become blind.' ⁴⁰Some of the Pharisees near him heard this, and they said to him, 'Are we also blind?' ⁴¹Jesus said to them, 'If you were blind, you would have no guilt; but now that you say, "We see," your guilt remains.'

The clash between the blind beggar who has been healed by Jesus and the Jewish leaders throws light upon another problem. This was expressed by a young ballet student who had recently come to faith in Jesus Christ. She once asked me rather sadly, 'Why are there not more Christians in the world?' We might also ask, why did so few people believe in Jesus in spite of His claims, His miracles, and the obvious attractiveness of His life? Part of the answer is to be found in the rest of this chapter. Physical blindness is a great tragedy. This story shows us that spiritual blindness is a greater one. Jesus comes to give light and sight to all who want it. But many people remain spiritually blind. Here are some of the marks of the spiritually blind.

a. They put prejudice before facts

The evidence was strong that this man had been healed by Jesus. Some of his neighbours recognized him (verse 8). He himself repeatedly stated that he was the man (verses 9b, 11, 15, 25, 30), in spite of the fact that his insistence led to excommunication (verse 34), and he had nothing to gain in sticking to his story if it was not true. The parents of the man also confirmed the fact that this man had been born blind and was indeed their son. It is astonishing that in the light of these facts the Pharisees were still prepared to deny that Jesus had given this man sight.

The reason is plain—and it is true of many people today. Men are prejudiced against facts when they are not convenient to them. The Jews were also prejudiced against Jesus. Jesus did not interpret the laws of the sabbath as they did (verse 16). He was not a follower of Moses, as they were (verse 28), nor did He have theological qualifications or the right social background (verse 29). They implied, without evidence, that He was morally suspect (verse 16). They were jealous of His influence upon the people (verse 22). They had no arguments to offer against the evidence of the man himself, and so resorted, not to reason, but to slander (verse 16), dangerous assertion (verse 24) and blustering anger (verse 34). It is a dangerous thing to put prejudice before facts. It is a mark of spiritual blindness. The case for Christianity does not rest on prejudice but on facts.

b. They put half-truths before the whole truth

As we have noticed before (John 6), the Jews had taken away from the real value of the sabbath, as a day of rest and worship and service, by the absurdity of their traditions. 'It was a sabbath day when Jesus made the clay and opened his eyes' (verse 14). Respect for the sabbath was important. It was part of God's law. 'The sabbath was made for man'—for his benefit. The Pharisees had half the truth in desiring to keep the sabbath as a different day; but a half-truth is often dangerous. The whole truth is that the sabbath is made for man. To heal a man kept the spirit of it completely. This the Pharisees failed to see. Sometimes a man fails to follow Jesus Christ today by saying 'religion is a personal matter', and so refusing to discuss it with anyone else. This is half the truth. Christianity is personal, but not secret. We need to beware of half-truths. They can sometimes keep us from seeing and believing in Jesus Christ.

c. They put argument before action

These men were constantly arguing and never coming to a decision (verses 24–38). They were always asking questions, but never *wanting* to find the answer. When the man asked the shrewd question 'Do you too *want* to become his disciples?' (verse 27), he hit the nail on the head. It is possible to engage in religious discussion with no intention of finding the truth. This man of course spoke from experience and not from theory. He could say, 'Though I was blind, now I see.' Indeed, this story makes plain that because this man wanted to know the truth about Christ, and because he was willing to believe and follow up such truth as he knew, his eyes were opened more and more to see who Jesus really was. First he spoke of Jesus as 'a man called Jesus' (verse 11), then 'a prophet' (verse 17). Then when Jesus asked him outright, 'Do you believe in the Son of man?' his willingness to follow the truth wherever it might lead is clear: ' "Who is he, sir, that I may believe in him?" Jesus said to him, "You have seen him, and it is he who speaks to you." *He said, "Lord, I believe"; and he worshipped him.*' In contrast, many of the Jews found it easier to argue than to act. It is easier to discuss than to decide to follow Christ. But the easy way is the way of spiritual blindness.

d. They put pride before humility

Pride is the basic cause of spiritual blindness. When a man stands before Jesus there is judgment on his pride (verse 39). Jesus came to give sight to the blind. The man who had been born with physical blindness discovered physical and spiritual sight in trusting and obeying Jesus Christ. Those who had physical sight in this story became even more spiritually blind by their repeated rejection of the facts, and especially of Jesus Himself. Their blindness was no accident. It could not be blamed on their environment. Although they too were blind from birth in a spiritual sense, in that they inherited a sinful human nature, they were also blind because of their deliberate self-righteousness and pride. 'Now that you say, "*We see*," your guilt remains.' If we would see Jesus and know Him to be all He claims to be, we must first of all humbly acknowledge our blindness and pride. To say that 'all is well' when I am blind to the truth of Jesus Christ is a mark of spiritual blindness.

23 JESUS, THE GOOD SHEPHERD
10:1–21

1 'Truly, truly, I say to you, he who does not enter the sheep-fold by the door but climbs in by another way, that man is a thief and a robber; ²but he who enters by the door is the shepherd of the sheep. ³To him the gate-keeper opens; the sheep hear his voice, and he calls his own sheep by name and leads them out. ⁴When he has brought out all his own, he goes before them, and the sheep follow him, for they know his voice. ⁵A stranger they will not follow, but they will flee from him, for they do not know the voice of strangers.' ⁶This figure Jesus used with them, but they did not understand what he was saying to them.

7 So Jesus again said to them, 'Truly, truly, I say to you, I am the door of the sheep. ⁸All who came before me are thieves and robbers; but the sheep did not heed them. ⁹I am the door; if any one enters by me, he will be saved, and will go in and out and find pasture. ¹⁰The thief comes only to steal and kill and destroy; I came that they may have life, and have it abundantly. ¹¹I am the good shepherd. The good shepherd lays

down his life for the sheep. ¹²He who is a hireling and not a shepherd, whose own the sheep are not, sees the wolf coming and leaves the sheep and flees; and the wolf snatches them and scatters them. ¹³He flees because he is a hireling and cares nothing for the sheep. ¹⁴I am the good shepherd; I know my own and my own know me, ¹⁵as the Father knows me and I know the Father; and I lay down my life for the sheep. ¹⁶And I have other sheep, that are not of this fold; I must bring them also, and they will heed my voice. So there shall be one flock, one shepherd. ¹⁷For this reason the Father loves me, because I lay down my life, that I may take it again. ¹⁸No one takes it from me, but I lay it down of my own accord. I have power to lay it down, and I have power to take it again; this charge I have received from my Father.'

19 There was again a division among the Jews because of these words. ²⁰Many of them said, 'He has a demon, and he is mad; why listen to him?' ²¹Others said, 'These are not the sayings of one who has a demon. Can a demon open the eyes of the blind?'

Judea was a pastoral rather than an agricultural country. No flock of sheep would graze without a shepherd or shepherds in attendance, so when Jesus referred to Himself as the good shepherd (verse 11) nothing could have been more familiar or topical. The Jew could understand this term in a number of ways.

In the Old Testament, God was sometimes referred to as the Shepherd of His people (see Psalm 80:1). Was Jesus then claiming to be God by using this phrase? Isaiah had spoken of God's 'Anointed One' as someone who would 'feed his flock like a shepherd' (Isaiah 40:11). Jeremiah referred to the unfaithful leaders of Israel as shepherds (Jeremiah 23:1–4).

But quite apart from these Old Testament allusions, there is something very attractive about the eastern shepherd. Dr. William Barclay* quotes the late Sir George Adam Smith's words about the shepherds of Palestine. 'On some high moor, across which at night the hyaenas howl, when you meet him (the shepherd), sleepless, far-sighted, weather-beaten, leaning on his staff, and looking out over his scattered sheep, every one of them on his heart, you understand why the shepherd of Judaea sprang to the front in his people's history; why they gave his name to their king, and made

* W. Barclay, *Daily Bible Readings: The Gospel of John*, vol. 2, p. 61.

him the symbol of providence; why Christ took him as the type of self-sacrifice.'

Jesus said, 'I am the good shepherd.' 'Good' here means literally 'attractive' (Greek *kalos*). There is nothing weak and feeble and anaemic about this picture of Christ. This is not the 'pale Galilaean' or the 'Gentle Jesus, meek and mild' of the sentimentalist. This is an attractive picture of someone who was watchful, resourceful and courageous, and yet loving, patient and sacrificial too.

We shall see the force of this description still more if we remember two further factors. First, Palestine sheep were mostly kept for their wool, whereas today they are very often kept for their meat as well. Eastern shepherds, therefore, would stay longer with their sheep and a close relationship between shepherd and sheep often developed. The shepherd knew his sheep by name (verse 3), and sheep were able to distinguish between the voice of the shepherd and the stranger (verses 3–5).

Second, in Palestine the shepherd leads his sheep from one sheep-fold to another over difficult and dangerous country. He does not drive them and chivvy them as elsewhere. In some villages, the shepherd might be able to leave his sheep for the night in a well-built communal sheep-fold which would have a door and even a door-keeper (see verses 1–4). But usually, as he led his sheep over the rough ground on the Judean plateau, the only sheep-fold for the night was a roughly-made wall, and the shepherd himself was the door (verse 7), lying down across the narrow opening to the fold, ready to defend his flock (verses 8–15).

Many of the Jews who listened to Jesus were longing for a leader, a shepherd, to guide them and protect them. As Jesus Himself once said, 'they were like sheep without a shepherd' (Mark 6:34). Much of the unrest in the world today is for precisely the same reason. A young person said recently, 'The world is looking for a leader.' When Jesus said to the crowds 'I am the good shepherd', He was promising to be a leader to His people and to give them security, satisfaction and unity.

a. Security

'I am the door,' said Jesus; 'if any one enters by me, he will be saved.' Sheep need the security of the sheep-fold. Many of the Jews had no sense of security. Politically, they were an occupied country. Religiously, their leaders were like the hired shepherds, who were more interested in their pay packet than the well-being of their flock (verse 11). The 'thieves and robbers' (verse 8) may refer to the false messiahs and false prophets who were trying to steal away their people from a true relationship with God. There is no security in religious leaders who have not come to Christ (verses 7, 8) and who destroy a man's relationship to Jesus Christ by destructive teaching and inconsistent lives. Nor is there security in those 'false messiahs' who promise a new age, or an exciting life apart from Jesus Christ. Men make many such promises today in the name of Communism, Humanism, Mormonism, or some other philosophy of life. Jesus teaches us that there is no security apart from Him. When we belong to Jesus Christ we shall hear His voice, and He will speak to us personally (verse 3), and lead us and go before us (verse 4), and we shall know His voice, and know when others would draw us away (verse 5). This security and safety in Jesus Christ is possible only because 'the good shepherd lays down his life for the sheep'.

b. Satisfaction

It is well known that those who attack Christianity will often do so on the grounds that it is narrow and that if a person becomes a Christian they will forfeit their enjoyment of life.

Jesus says the opposite is true. Those who try to draw us away from Him are those who come 'to steal and kill and destroy' (verse 10). A girl persuaded against her better judgment to commit immorality does not thereby enter into a fully satisfying new life. Indeed the experience of those who have fallen in this particular way is that something good has been 'lost, killed and destroyed'. Those who come to Jesus, on the other hand, are promised the security of being saved or delivered from spiritual death (verse 9) and the satisfaction of going 'in and out to find pasture'. 'I came', said Jesus, 'that they may have life, and have it abundantly' (verse

10). A member of our church congregation wrote: 'Having been brought up on the philosophy "eat, drink and be merry, for tomorrow we die" I was determined to get the most out of life. I joined clubs, went to all-night parties and lived in a constant whirl of social activity. To my friends I really seemed to be "living", but deep down inside I knew it wasn't true. I became more and more dissatisfied and life seemed pointless. Then I heard about the new life that Christ offered. Somehow I knew this was what I needed and so I asked Him into my life to renew it and redirect it. Since then I have known increasing satisfaction and fulfilment more than I had ever known before.' As we follow the Shepherd, however hard the way, He will lead us on to find more and more satisfaction in Him.

c. Unity

Jesus was not only concerned about those already in the Jewish fold. He was concerned about those who were outside organized religion—the Gentiles. 'I have other sheep, that are not of this fold; I must bring them also, and they will heed my voice. So there shall be one flock, one shepherd' (verse 16).

Jesus lived in a divided world even as we do. The Jew hated and despised the Gentile. But Jesus came to bring men together by bringing them, first, not into the same 'fold', but into the same flock—that is, in relationship to Himself, the good Shepherd. In laying down His life for all men (verse 18) He was to break down barriers that divide men from one another. But the same Christ who unites those who believe in Him, divides those who cannot make up their minds about Him. Once again the issue is raised, 'Is He deluded or divine?' (verses 19–21).

22 It was the feast of the Dedication at Jerusalem; ²³it was winter, and Jesus was walking in the temple, in the portico of Solomon. ²⁴So the Jews gathered round him and said to him, 'How long will you keep us in suspense? If you are the Christ, tell us plainly.' ²⁵Jesus answered them, 'I told you, and you do not believe. The works that I do in my Father's name, they bear witness to me; ²⁶but you do not believe, because you do not belong to my sheep. ²⁷My sheep hear my voice, and I know them, and they follow me; ²⁸and I give them eternal life, and they shall never perish; and no one shall snatch them out of my hand. ²⁹My Father, who has given them to me, is greater than all, and no one is able to snatch them out of the Father's hand. ³⁰I and the Father are one.'

31 The Jews took up stones again to stone him. ³²Jesus answered them, 'I have shown you many good works from the Father; for which of these do you stone me?' ³³The Jews answered him, 'We stone you for no good work but for blasphemy; because you, being a man, make yourself God.' ³⁴Jesus answered them, 'Is it not written in your law, "I said, you are gods"? ³⁵If he called them gods to whom the word of God came (and scripture cannot be broken), ³⁶do you say of him whom the Father consecrated and sent into the world, "You are blaspheming," because I said, "I am the Son of God"? ³⁷If I am not doing the works of my Father, then do not believe me; ³⁸but if I do them, even though you do not believe me, believe the works, that you may know and understand that the Father is in me and I am in the Father.' ³⁹Again they tried to arrest him, but he escaped from their hands.

40 He went away again across the Jordan to the place where John at first baptized, and there he remained. ⁴¹And many came to him; and they said, 'John did no sign, but everything that John said about this man was true.' ⁴²And many believed in him there.

It was a time of national thanksgiving. The Feast of the Dedication (verse 22) commemorated the epic victory of the freedom fighters

under Judas Maccabaeus in 164 BC. The Temple had been dese-
crated by the enemies of the Jews; but in 164 BC it was ceremonially
cleansed and purified, and Judas Maccabaeus ordered that 'the days
of the dedication of the altar should be kept in their season from
year to year, by the space of eight days, from the five and twentieth
day of the month of Chislev, with gladness and joy' (1 Maccabees
4:59).

This Festival was also called the Festival of Lights, and illu-
minations would be seen in the Temple and in every Jewish home,
as a reminder that the light of freedom had come back to Israel.
It was during this Festival, in the winter, that Jesus walked in the
Temple, in the place (Solomon's portico) where Rabbis would
often talk with their students. It is doubtful whether the questions
of the Jews were really sincere; but this incident shows Jesus'
patience with His enemies and His love for His disciples.

a. His patience with His enemies

The Jewish leaders ask for plain speaking, but are probably trying
to trap Jesus in His speech so that they can arrest Him (verse 39).
Jesus is amazingly patient with them, and continues to give them
evidence for His claims. Once again He urges them to consider
His works (verse 25) and *His words* (verse 27). When they argue
that His words are blasphemous, for He claims to be God (verse
33), Jesus tries to help them take a more reasonable attitude. He
argues from the Old Testament Scriptures in a way that would be
familiar to them. The Jews believed, as Jesus did, that the Scriptures (Old Testament) were completely reliable (verse 35). Yet in
the Old Testament the writer of Psalm 82 had called some unjust
judges 'gods'. For a judge is commissioned by God to bring God's
help and justice to men. He is God to men (see Psalm 82). Jesus
argues that if Scripture can speak like that about men who are set
apart for a special task by God, how much more should they be
willing to call Jesus God, who has so obviously been sent by God
into this world for a unique purpose, as His words and works bear
witness.

Furthermore, even if they cannot accept this verbal argument,
surely the life of Jesus and His works are clear enough evidence of

His unique relationship to His Father? Surely only the Son of God, someone equal with God, could do such mighty works?

Some men will not listen to Jesus, however patiently and logically He states His case. The Jews did not belong to Jesus and so would not believe Him. They had no arguments against His case, no real reasons to reject Him. So they tried force (verse 39). But some believed, some realized that Jesus practised what He preached. John the Baptist had done no 'signs' (verse 41). Jesus had done many. Some began to realize that everything that the Baptist said about Jesus was true. But they could only be sure of this when they came to Jesus (verse 41) and believed in Him (verse 42).

b. His love for His disciples (verses 27–30)

Yet again Jesus uses the picture of the shepherd's love for the sheep in describing His relationship with believers. Once a believer has come to the good Shepherd, he is able to recognize the voice of Jesus, and to know that His words are reliable. He enters into a relationship with Jesus. Jesus can say 'I know him', and he is able to follow Jesus. Jesus gives His disciples eternal life and promises them eternal security. This security is based on His Father's love as well as His own (verses 28, 29).

Some people go through life never knowing whether they have eternal life or not, and uncertain of their future destiny. Jesus says that those who believe on Him may be certain of eternal security—'they shall never perish, and no one shall snatch them out of my hand.'

It is interesting to compare these sure promises of Jesus with the uncertainties of many of our modern thinkers. In *A Writer's Notebook*, Somerset Maugham comments on Bertrand Russell's philosophy.* 'It may be that, as he (Russell) says, philosophy doesn't offer or attempt to offer a solution of the problems of human destiny; it may be that it mustn't hope to find an answer to the practical problems of life; for philosophers have other fish to fry. But who then will tell us whether there is any sense in living, and whether human existence is anything but a tragic—no, tragic is too noble a word—whether human existence is anything but a grotesque

* W. Somerset Maugham, *A Writer's Notebook*, p. 313.

mischance?' One can only wish that Maugham had pondered the words of Jesus as much as the philosophy of Russell. There is nothing aimless or uncertain for those who follow the good Shepherd throughout their life.

25 THE RAISING OF LAZARUS
11 : 1–53

1 Now a certain man was ill, Lazarus of Bethany, the village of Mary and her sister Martha. ²It was Mary who anointed the Lord with ointment and wiped his feet with her hair, whose brother Lazarus was ill. ³So the sisters sent to him, saying, 'Lord, he whom you love is ill.' ⁴But when Jesus heard it he said, 'This illness is not unto death; it is for the glory of God, so that the Son of God may be glorified by means of it.'
5 Now Jesus loved Martha and her sister and Lazarus. ⁶So when he heard that he was ill, he stayed two days longer in the place where he was. ⁷Then after this he said to the disciples, 'Let us go into Judea again.' ⁸The disciples said to him, 'Rabbi, the Jews were but now seeking to stone you, and are you going there again?' ⁹Jesus answered, 'Are there not twelve hours in the day? If any one walks in the day, he does not stumble, because he sees the light of this world. ¹⁰But if any one walks in the night, he stumbles, because the light is not in him.' ¹¹Thus he spoke, and then he said to them, 'Our friend Lazarus has fallen asleep, but I go to awake him out of sleep.' ¹²The disciples said to him, 'Lord, if he has fallen asleep, he will recover.' ¹³Now Jesus had spoken of his death, but they thought that he meant taking rest in sleep. ¹⁴Then Jesus told them plainly, 'Lazarus is dead; ¹⁵and for your sake I am glad that I was not there, so that you may believe. But let us go to him.' ¹⁶Thomas, called the Twin, said to his fellow disciples, 'Let us also go, that we may die with him.'
17 Now when Jesus came, he found that Lazarus had already been in the tomb four days. ¹⁸Bethany was near Jerusalem, about two miles off, ¹⁹and many of the Jews had come to Martha and Mary to console them concerning their brother. ²⁰When

Martha heard that Jesus was coming, she went and met him, while Mary sat in the house. ²¹Martha said to Jesus, 'Lord, if you had been here, my brother would not have died. ²²And even now I know that whatever you ask from God, God will give you.' ²³Jesus said to her, 'Your brother will rise again.' ²⁴Martha said to him, 'I know that he will rise again in the resurrection at the last day.' ²⁵Jesus said to her, 'I am the resurrection and the life; he who believes in me, though he die, yet shall he live, ²⁶and whoever lives and believes in me shall never die. Do you believe this?' ²⁷She said to him, 'Yes, Lord; I believe that you are the Christ, the Son of God, he who is coming into the world.'

28 When she had said this, she went and called her sister Mary, saying quietly, 'The Teacher is here and is calling for you.' ²⁹And when she heard it, she rose quickly and went to him. ³⁰Now Jesus had not yet come to the village, but was still in the place where Martha had met him. ³¹When the Jews who were with her in the house, consoling her, saw Mary rise quickly and go out, they followed her, supposing that she was going to the tomb to weep there. ³²Then Mary, when she came where Jesus was and saw him, fell at his feet, saying to him, 'Lord, if you had been here, my brother would not have died.' ³³When Jesus saw her weeping, and the Jews who came with her also weeping, he was deeply moved in spirit and troubled; ³⁴and he said, 'Where have you laid him?' They said to him, 'Lord, come and see.' ³⁵Jesus wept. ³⁶So the Jews said, 'See how he loved him!' ³⁷But some of them said, 'Could not he who opened the eyes of the blind man have kept this man from dying?'

38 Then Jesus, deeply moved again, came to the tomb; it was a cave, and a stone lay upon it. ³⁹Jesus said, 'Take away the stone.' Martha, the sister of the dead man, said to him, 'Lord, by this time there will be an odour, for he has been dead four days.' ⁴⁰Jesus said to her, 'Did I not tell you that if you would believe you would see the glory of God?' ⁴¹So they took away the stone. And Jesus lifted up his eyes and said, 'Father, I thank thee that thou hast heard me. ⁴²I knew that thou hearest me always, but I have said this on account of the people standing by, that they may believe that thou didst send me.' ⁴³When he had said this, he cried with a loud voice, 'Lazarus, come out.' ⁴⁴The dead man came out, his hands and feet bound with bandages, and his face wrapped with a cloth. Jesus said to them, 'Unbind him, and let him go.'

45 Many of the Jews therefore, who had come with Mary and had seen what he did, believed in him; ⁴⁶but some of them went to the Pharisees and told them what Jesus had done. ⁴⁷So the

chief priests and the Pharisees gathered the council, and said, 'What are we to do? For this man performs many signs. ⁴⁸If we let him go on thus, every one will believe in him, and the Romans will come and destroy both our holy place and our nation.' ⁴⁹But one of them, Caiaphas, who was high priest that year, said to them, 'You know nothing at all; ⁵⁰you do not understand that it is expedient for you that one man should die for the people, and not that the whole nation should perish.' ⁵¹He did not say this of his own accord, but being high priest that year he prophesied that Jesus should die for the nation, ⁵²and not for the nation only, but to gather into one the children of God who are scattered abroad. ⁵³So from that day on they took counsel how to put him to death.

'Now a certain man was ill, Lazarus of Bethany.' The illness of a great friend of Jesus, who lived with his two sisters in the village of Bethany, is the occasion of one of the most astonishing signs in the ministry of Jesus. Bethany was only a few miles out from Jerusalem, not far from where opposition to Jesus' ministry was increasing. In this story we learn how 'unanswered prayer', sickness, death and bereavement can be used to uphold the reputation of God and strengthen the faith of disciples. The purpose of this event is expressed in the words of Jesus Himself: 'This illness is not unto death; it is for the glory of God, so that the Son of God may be glorified by means of it.' Later, Jesus explains what He means more specifically by saying, 'Lazarus is dead; and for your sake I am glad that I was not there, so that you may believe.' These apparently calamitous events strengthened the faith of those involved.

a. The disciples' faith in the wisdom of Jesus

When the message comes to Jesus that Lazarus is seriously ill, we read the unlikely comment, 'So when he heard that he was ill, he stayed two days longer in the place where he was.' By the time, therefore, that Jesus reached Bethany, Lazarus had died. At first the disciples could not understand this at all. Furthermore, when Jesus announced that He was going to Bethany, the disciples believed that they would be walking into further trouble (verse 8). Sometimes God's actions are baffling even to the believer.

> 'God moves in a mysterious way,
> His wonders to perform.'

But the disciples learnt that day at Bethany that even when a request is not immediately answered (verse 6), and when the way seems unnecessarily difficult and dangerous (verse 8), Jesus knows what He is doing. When we follow Him, we walk in the light and not in the darkness (verses 9, 10). He has a plan and a purpose even when sickness and death and bereavement afflict His friends. At first Thomas expresses only brave but pessimistic loyalty (verse 16). Later the faith of the disciples is strengthened as they discover the loving wisdom of Jesus Christ in all His actions. Christians can say, with the apostle Paul, that 'we know that in everything God works for good with those who love him, who are called according to his purpose' (see Romans 8:28).

b. Martha's faith in the authority of Jesus (verses 17–27)

Martha was shattered by the failure of Jesus to do what she asked. She could not resist reproaching Jesus: 'Lord, if you had been here, my brother would not have died' (verse 21). No doubt she felt the same as others who have prayed desperately that God would save a relative or a friend from death, only to find that God has not answered in that way. Martha, I imagine, is a busy, practical woman, who is not much given to deep thought or meditation. Her faith in Jesus is such that she still believes He can help them (verse 22). She can trot out the orthodox Jewish belief about the resurrection at the last day (verse 24). But there was no doubt a hollow sound about those words while the loss of her brother was so close. But Jesus is concerned to strengthen the faith of ordinary, practical men and women. Bereavement has caused her to think about life and death in a deeper way. She has yet to understand that Jesus can not only heal the sick, but He can also raise the dead. Indeed, to believe in Jesus is to experience spiritual life now and for ever. 'Whoever *lives* and *believes* in me shall never die.' At that moment of grief and sorrow Martha's faith in the authority and uniqueness of Jesus came to life. 'I believe,' she said, 'that you are the Christ, the Son of God, he who is coming into the world.'

c. Mary's faith in the love of Jesus (verses 28–37)

Mary was of a very different temperament from Martha. She preferred to stay at home, consoled by her friends, until Jesus called her. She, too, could not understand why Jesus had not come to Bethany sooner (verse 32). But if Jesus had not delayed His coming, Mary would not have seen that day how much Jesus understands human sorrow and suffering. For 'Jesus wept' (verse 35). No doubt His tears were in sorrow at the sense of desolation and loss that death brought to those who were still in the dark about the future life. No doubt He wept out of sympathy for His friends. This story assures the Christian that Jesus understands and cares about human sorrow. Like Mary, our faith in the love of Jesus can be strengthened in times of bereavement.

d. The crowd's faith in the power of Jesus (verses 38–57)

It is hard to imagine how men could begin to understand the power of Jesus over death and the grave unless He demonstrated this power in a sign of this kind. The other Gospels speak of Jesus raising people from the dead (see Matthew 9:18–26; Luke 7:11–17), but they do not in fact mention this remarkable story, which involves restoration—for the body had begun to decompose (verse 39). Jairus's daughter and the widow of Nain's son were raised soon after death. If Peter was not with the disciples at Bethany and if Peter's sermons and memoirs are one of the chief sources for Mark's Gospel, then this may explain the absence of this story from the Synoptic Gospels, for Matthew and Luke depend to some extent on Mark's record. Also, John is writing at a later date, when Lazarus is probably no longer alive. The story might have embarrassed Lazarus if he had been still alive. Certainly this description of the raising of Lazarus, simple and restrained as it is, has all the marks of an eyewitness account.

Jesus prayed (verses 41, 42) that people might know that God had sent Him—and then He demonstrated the power of God over death and the grave by summoning Lazarus back to life again (verses 43, 44). Jesus had thus authenticated His claim to be 'the resurrection and the life' (verse 25), which He proved conclusively by His own resurrection from the dead.

The attitude of Jesus Christ and His followers to death is one of the most distinctive marks of Christianity. Even the Jewish mourners, who believed in a resurrection of the just and the unjust (verse 24), would be beside themselves with grief when bereaved. As Dr. William Barclay expressed it: 'We must remember that this would be no gentle, restrained shedding of tears. It would be unrestrained wailing and shrieking almost hysterically, for it was the Jewish point of view that the more unrestrained the weeping was the more honour it paid to the dead.'*

Many of the Greeks would have agreed with Aristotle's words, 'Death is a dreadful thing, for it is the end.' In more modern times Rousseau said, 'He who pretends to face death without fear is a liar!' and Aldous Huxley once wrote, 'If you're a busy film-going, newspaper-reading, chocolate-eating modern, then death is hell.'

Jesus Christ, on the other hand, has demonstrated by this raising of Lazarus from the dead, and by His own resurrection, that death is not the end. Jesus describes death in terms of rest (verses 11–14) and life (verse 25). This is why the martyr Stephen could say, as the stones began to fly, 'Behold, I see the heavens opened, and the Son of man standing at the right hand of God' (Acts 7:56). Or Guthrie, the Scottish Covenanter, after he had wakened from a peaceful sleep on the morning of his execution, 'This is the day which the Lord hath made, we will rejoice and be glad in it.' D. L. Moody, the great American evangelist of the last century, once said, 'Some fine morning you will see in the newspapers, D. L. Moody is dead. Don't you believe it. I shall be more alive that morning than ever before.'

But if many believed in the power of Jesus that day at Bethany (verse 45), there were others who would not believe. Indeed a sign of this kind only increased their jealousy and fear and hatred (verses 46–53). John, however, reminds us again that God's purpose was being worked out in this, so that even a casual comment from the high priest, Caiaphas, has a deeper significance than he himself realized. Jesus was still moving forward to that hour when His death would be the means of uniting all believers (verses 50–52).

* W. Barclay, *Daily Bible Readings: The Gospel of John*, vol. 2, p. 112.

54 Jesus therefore no longer went about openly among the Jews, but went from there to the country near the wilderness, to a town called Ephraim; and there he stayed with the disciples.

55 Now the Passover of the Jews was at hand, and many went up from the country to Jerusalem before the Passover, to purify themselves. ⁵⁶They were looking for Jesus and saying to one another as they stood in the temple, 'What do you think? That he will not come to the feast?' ⁵⁷Now the chief priests and the Pharisees had given orders that if any one knew where he was, he should let them know, so that they might arrest him.

1 Six days before the Passover, Jesus came to Bethany, where Lazarus was, whom Jesus had raised from the dead. ²There they made him a supper; Martha served, and Lazarus was one of those at table with him.³ Mary took a pound of costly ointment of pure nard and anointed the feet of Jesus and wiped his feet with her hair; and the house was filled with the fragrance of the ointment. ⁴But Judas Iscariot, one of his disciples (he who was to betray him), said, ⁵'Why was this ointment not sold for three hundred denarii and given to the poor?' ⁶This he said, not that he cared for the poor but because he was a thief, and as he had the money box he used to take what was put into it. ⁷Jesus said, 'Let her alone, let her keep it for the day of my burial. ⁸The poor you always have with you, but you do not always have me.'

9 When the great crowd of the Jews learned that he was there, they came, not only on account of Jesus but also to see Lazarus, whom he had raised from the dead. ¹⁰So the chief priests planned to put Lazarus also to death, ¹¹because on account of him many of the Jews were going away and believing in Jesus.

12 The next day a great crowd who had come to the feast heard that Jesus was coming to Jerusalem. ¹³So they took branches of palm trees and went out to meet him, crying, 'Hosanna! Blessed is he who comes in the name of the Lord, even the King of Israel!' ¹⁴And Jesus found a young ass and sat upon it; as it is written,

15'Fear not, daughter of Zion;
behold, your king is coming,
sitting on an ass's colt!'

16His disciples did not understand this at first; but when Jesus
was glorified, then they remembered that this had been written
of him and had been done to him. 17The crowd that had been
with him when he called Lazarus out of the tomb and raised
him from the dead bore witness. 18The reason why the crowd
went to meet him was that they heard he had done this sign.
19The Pharisees then said to one another, 'You see that you can
do nothing; look, the world has gone after him.'

20 Now among those who went up to worship at the feast
were some Greeks. 21So these came to Philip, who was from
Bethsaida in Galilee, and said to him, 'Sir, we wish to see
Jesus.' 22Philip went and told Andrew; Andrew went with
Philip and they told Jesus. 23And Jesus answered them, 'The
hour has come for the Son of man to be glorified. 24Truly,
truly, I say to you, unless a grain of wheat falls into the earth
and dies, it remains alone; but if it dies, it bears much fruit.
25He who loves his life loses it, and he who hates his life in this
world will keep it for eternal life. 26If any one serves me, he must
follow me; and where I am, there shall my servant be also; if
any one serves me, the Father will honour him.'

When Jesus stayed with His friends, first at Ephraim, in the
mountainous country north-east of Jerusalem, and then at Bethany
with Lazarus, Martha and Mary, it became increasingly clear that
people had to take sides for or against Him. The raising of Lazarus
from the dead was either an act of God or magic. Lazarus was there
for all to see, and many came to see him, curious about the strange
event of his resurrection.

Jesus did not immediately walk into danger (verse 54), but it is
clear that He was quite prepared to declare Himself as Messiah
when the right moment came, whatever His enemies might say or
do (see verses 12–18). Again we notice that the reactions to Jesus
nearly 2,000 years ago were very similar to typical reactions to Him
today.

a. Some were curious about Jesus (verses 55, 56)

Before a Jew attended a feast he was obliged to be ceremonially
clean. Many Jewish pilgrims arrived in Jerusalem several days

before the Passover, so that they could attend to the various ceremonial and religious obligations. By this time Jerusalem was resounding with the name of Jesus. His reputation as a miracle-
worker and His clash with the religious authorities made Him an
exciting topic of conversation. But it is not sufficient merely to talk
about Jesus, if we would really know Him. For many in the crowd
curiosity did not lead to concern for the truth.

b. Mary lavished her love on Jesus (verses 1–3, 7, 8)

At Bethany, only six days before the Passover, Jesus was invited
back there for a meal, we may believe, prepared specially in His
honour. Martha, as always, was busy serving the meal. Lazarus sat at
table and talked with Jesus. Then Mary, quieter than her sister, but
capable of greater depths of love and loyalty, makes an extravagant
gesture of gratitude. She takes a pound of very costly ointment and
anoints Jesus with it. It is a spontaneous gesture which receives the
commendation of Jesus, for He sees that her heart has been touched
and her motives are the best. Love and loyalty to Jesus should
never be cold and calculating. We love Him because He first loved
us. The church of God needs more of those who will love Jesus
with reckless and extravagant love.

c. Judas loved money more than Jesus (verses 4–6)

The contrast between Judas and Mary is striking. It is the contrast
between belief and unbelief. We have here one of the clearest statements in the Gospels about the motives of Judas Iscariot, who later
betrayed Jesus (verse 6). The writer of this Gospel is quite clear
that Judas has used his position as treasurer in the band of disciples
to make money for himself. His disgruntled comment about Mary's
extravagance was therefore both hypocritical and deceitful. Maybe
Judas's dissatisfaction was partly because Jesus gave no indication
that He was prepared to bring off a political coup which would
have suited Judas's materialistic attitude better. But his words
(verse 5) about giving 'to the poor' warn us that it is easy enough
to excuse our lack of love for Jesus by pretending we want to give
to some good cause. We cannot buy off our responsibility to Jesus

Christ by acts of charity. Neither can we serve both Christ *and* money.

d. The chief priests threatened to kill Jesus (verses 9–11)

Their motives too are clear. They are jealous of the influence that Jesus has over the crowds (verses 10, 11, 19), and they have no answer to the claims that Jesus makes. There are always men who will utterly oppose Christianity through jealousy and resentment.

e. The crowds are prepared to shout for Jesus (verses 12–19)

In describing the entry of Jesus into Jerusalem, John does not mention the way in which the disciples first went to prepare for the Passover meal, which the other Gospels describe. John's interest is in the response of the crowds. 'Hosanna' means 'save, we pray'; and the shouting of this word and the quotation from Psalm 118, which was one of the Psalms sung at the Passover in anticipation of the coming of the Messiah, show that many people were prepared to accept Jesus as the Messiah. We cannot be sure whether their ideas about the Messiah were still only political and materialistic; but Jesus goes out of His way to emphasize that He comes to Jerusalem as a king of peace in fulfilment of the Old Testament Scriptures. Judges and kings usually rode on donkeys (verses 14, 15) on errands of peace, and on horseback in time of war. It is easier to shout for a Christ who brings material and political improvements than for a king who suffers in order to establish a spiritual kingdom. But the New Testament constantly reminds us that there can be no peace and prosperity amongst men unless there is first peace with God. The disciples understood the full significance of this only after the death and resurrection of Jesus (verse 16).

f. The Greeks wanted to see Jesus (verses 20–26)

The Greeks who came to Jerusalem were probably Jewish proselytes, or converts to Judaism. They found the revealed religion of the Jews more satisfying than pagan superstitions. But the appeal of Jesus is more satisfying still. One of the disciples, Philip, had a

Greek name, and was probably born in a Greek-speaking community. Perhaps it was for this reason that the Greeks first approached Philip, who then cautiously asks Andrew's advice. Together they go to Jesus, and we assume that they introduced the enquiring Greeks to Him. Certainly Jesus was concerned for Greeks as well as Jews. But He was also concerned that those who sought to follow Him should understand the nature of His mission and the cost of discipleship. So Jesus emphasizes two important principles.

1. *For Jesus—the way of life is through death* (verses 23, 24). The moment when Jesus will be most honoured will not be when Jews and Gentiles flock to see Him, but when, like a grain of wheat, He dies as a prelude to rising again and giving life to many. Nature is a constant reminder to us that death is a necessary prelude to life (verse 24). It was necessary for Jesus to die, if we are to live.

2. *For the disciple—the way of life is through death* (verses 25, 26). The disciple of Jesus Christ is called to die to self and to live for Christ. If his love for Christ is such that in comparison his love for himself is like hatred, then he will enjoy God's gift of eternal life. Negatively, he must hate self-centred living and, positively, he must serve Christ. The rewards of such unselfish service will be the presence of Christ and the honour of God (verse 26).

The story of Jim Vaus, a notorious criminal wire-tapper in America, converted under the preaching of Dr. Billy Graham a few years ago, illustrates this change of attitude from self-centredness to unselfish service. After Vaus had begun to follow Christ, a man came to him willing to pay $10,000 for information that would settle a case of libel. Jim Vaus speaks: 'Evidently you haven't heard.' 'Haven't heard what?' the man replies. Jim Vaus answers, 'Jim Vaus is dead.' Vaus describes the man's reactions: 'The man's eyes bulged, his chin dropped, and he looked as if I'd lost my mind.' 'That's right', said Vaus, 'the man you are looking for, who used to tap wires, make recordings and sell them to the highest bidder, is dead. I'm a new man, because the Bible says, "If any man be in Christ he is a new creation".'* Jesus Christ calls His disciples to die to the old self-centred sinful life, and to live for Him in daily sacrificial service.

* Jim Vaus, *Why I quit syndicated crime.*

27 'Now is my soul troubled. And what shall I say? "Father, save me from this hour"? No, for this purpose I have come to this hour. 28Father, glorify thy name.' Then a voice came from heaven, 'I have glorified it, and I will glorify it again.' 29The crowd standing by heard it and said that it had thundered. Others said, 'An angel has spoken to him.' 30Jesus answered, 'This voice has come for your sake, not for mine. 31Now is the judgment of this world, now shall the ruler of this world be cast out; 32and I, when I am lifted up from the earth, will draw all men to myself.' 33He said this to show by what death he was to die. 34The crowd answered him, 'We have heard from the law that the Christ remains for ever. How can you say that the Son of man must be lifted up? Who is this Son of man?' 35Jesus said to them, 'The light is with you for a little longer. Walk while you have the light, lest the darkness overtake you; he who walks in the darkness does not know where he goes. 36While you have the light, believe in the light, that you may become sons of light.'

When Jesus had said this, he departed and hid himself from them. 37Though he had done so many signs before them, yet they did not believe in him; 38it was that the word spoken by the prophet Isaiah might be fulfilled:

'Lord, who has believed our report,
    and to whom has the arm of the Lord been revealed?'

39Therefore they could not believe. For Isaiah again said,

40'He has blinded their eyes and hardened their heart,
    lest they should see with their eyes and perceive with
        their heart,
    and turn for me to heal them.'

41Isaiah said this because he saw his glory and spoke of him. 42Nevertheless many even of the authorities believed in him, but for fear of the Pharisees they did not confess it, lest they should be put out of the synagogue; 43for they loved the praise of men more than the praise of God.

44 And Jesus cried out and said, 'He who believes in me, believes not in me but in him who sent me. ⁴⁵And he who sees me sees him who sent me. ⁴⁶I have come as light into the world, that whoever believes in me may not remain in darkness. ⁴⁷If any one hears my sayings and does not keep them, I do not judge him; for I did not come to judge the world but to save the world. ⁴⁸He who rejects me and does not receive my sayings has a judge; the word that I have spoken will be his judge on the last day. ⁴⁹For I have not spoken on my own authority; the Father who sent me has himself given me commandment what to say and what to speak. ⁵⁰And I know that his commandment is eternal life. What I say, therefore, I say as the Father has bidden me.'

Sometimes people are surprised and even offended that the death of Jesus is so central and important in Christianity. The symbol of Christianity is a cross. The story of the death of Jesus in the Gospels takes up a disproportionate amount of space compared with other biographies. Some modern thinkers would even like to dismiss this teaching about the death of Christ, with its emphasis upon blood and sacrifice, as 'a hangover from a primitive blood ritual'. But the visit of the Greeks to Jesus provides an occasion for Jesus Himself to tell us how central in His own thinking is His death.

a. The importance of His death (verse 27)

In His real humanity, Jesus naturally shrinks from the prospect of physical suffering and death. 'Now is my soul troubled. And what shall I say? "Father, save me from this hour"?' Jesus is one of us. He understands and has shared this instinctive reaction to suffering. But He also acknowledges that He has come into this world to die. This is the chief purpose of His coming. This is 'the hour' which is to be the climax of His life and ministry.

b. The glory of His death (verses 28, 29)

There is little doubt that the disciples of Jesus as well as others would regard His death as shameful and a terrible disgrace. Jesus knows it will be the moment when God is honoured and glorified. For Jesus, the glory of God matters. It is doing God's will, even if it leads to death on a Roman gibbet, that brings glory to God. The voice from heaven, which appears to be no more than a clap of thunder to those whose ears are not attuned to God, assures the crowds and Jesus Himself that such a life of obedience has already brought honour to God, and will do so again.

c. The victory of His death (verses 30, 31)

In the eyes of the world the death of Christ appeared to be a tragic failure, a defeat. Jesus knew that in the plan of God it was to be a great victory. The 'ruler of this world', a title emphasizing the great power of the devil, would be cast out, and the selfishness and sin of the world would be judged.

Men sometimes ask why evil is so rampant today. In the last World War the victory at Normandy was decisive in the eventual victory of the Allies. However, there was much further fighting and mopping up that needed to be completed before final victory came. The death of Christ was decisive in the overthrow of Satan. We must wait until Jesus Christ comes again at the end of the world for the complete victory to be accomplished and enjoyed.

d. The power of His death (verses 32, 33)

For some people the death of Christ seems to be nonsense, and because of man's pride it is sometimes a stumbling-block (see 1 Corinthians 1:23, 24). For it tells us that God has had to do something about man's rebellion and sin, and that man cannot save himself. However, the Christian knows that his sins are forgiven and that God accepts him because of the death of Christ. It is the love of God revealed supremely in Christ's death for sinners that draws a man to God. Jesus here predicts that it will be as a consequence of His being 'lifted up' to die on the cross that men will be drawn to Him.

This was the experience of a man who served as a pilot and commissioned flying instructor during World War II and who then went up to Cambridge to take his degree. He was invited to a mission service that was being held under the auspices of the Cambridge Inter-Collegiate Christian Union. He writes, 'One evening the address was on Isaiah 53, and then for the first time I realized that Christ's death on the cross affected me personally. "He was wounded for *my* transgressions, he was bruised for *my* iniquities . . . with his stripes *I* am healed." I certainly had no overwhelming sense of sin, and I reckoned that I had lived a normal, decent sort of life. But I knew, too, that I had never really thanked Christ for what He had done for me on the cross, and that ingratitude was just a form of sin. As I thanked Him that night, and offered Him my life in gratitude, a sense of assurance came to me, based not on any feelings, and certainly not on any sense of worthiness, but on the written Word of God. I knew that I was now saved, not because of anything that I had done, but because Jesus Christ had done all that was necessary for my salvation.'* The message of the death of Christ still draws people today.

e. Reactions to the message of His death (verses 34–43)

There is more than one way to react to the message of Christ's death, as these next verses make clear.

1. *Some did not understand* (verses 34–36). Some could not believe in a *Messiah* that would have to die (verse 33). Should not the Messiah live for ever? Again, the 'Son of man' described in Daniel 7:13 would come in glory 'with the clouds of heaven'. Who, then, is this 'Son of man' who speaks of this glory of death by crucifixion? Jesus implies that if only they were willing, He would give them understanding and take away their ignorance. 'While you have the light (that is, the Christ amongst them), *believe* in the light, that you may become *sons of light*.' We shall never fully understand the meaning of the death of Christ with out finite minds. But if we look to Christ and listen to Him we shall find sufficient light to walk by.

2. *Some would not believe* (verses 37–41). In spite of the miracles and signs of Jesus many reacted to Jesus in the same way as many had reacted earlier to the prophet Isaiah. Indeed, Isaiah had foreseen that when the Messiah came many would be too blind to see Him, and too hardened to respond to Him. The writers in the Bible sometimes spoke of *God* hardening men's hearts. When the Pharaoh

* W. F. Batt (editor), *Facing the Facts*, p. 60.

of Egypt had repeatedly rejected the message from God which he heard from the lips of Moses, it was finally said 'and God hardened Pharaoh's heart' (see Exodus 7–11). There comes a moment when persistent rejection of God's Word leads to such hardness of heart that God is not willing to speak any more. Paul uses the phrase, *'God gave them up* to a base mind' (Romans 1:28). The more we reject God's Word the harder our hearts become. That is why there is often a note of urgency in the Bible, when men are exhorted to turn from their sins to God. 'Now is the acceptable time; behold, now is the day of salvation' (2 Corinthians 6:2).

3. *Some believed in secret* (verses 42, 43). Jesus once said that if we were to be ashamed of Him in this life, He would be ashamed of us in the next life (Mark 8:38). John tells us that many people, even those in important and responsible positions in society, did not reject Christ but were ashamed to acknowledge Him publicly. Why should men want to be only secret disciples? John's answer is: (i) *They feared men's opinions*. These men were afraid of the Pharisees. Fear of what others will think often keeps a man from confessing he is a Christian. (ii) *They loved men's praise*. These men were not prepared to be thrown out of the synagogue, isolated from their group in society. They did not want to lose their friends or their comfortable niche in society. John sums up their position by saying of them what, sadly, can often be said of us: 'they loved the praise of men more than the praise of God.'

f. What is our response to Jesus and His message? (verses 44–50)

In the last verses of this chapter Jesus once again makes the issue clear. To believe in Jesus is to believe in God. To see Jesus as the Son of God and Saviour of sinners is to see God. To believe on Him is to walk in the knowledge of God and not in ignorance. It is to walk in the light and not darkness. But what if we hear this message and reject it? Jesus told the Pharisees that His coming into this world was primarily for salvation and not judgment (verse 47). But one day He will come to judge the world, and on that day our salvation, our acceptance with God, will depend on our attitude and response to the divine and authoritative words of Jesus Christ,

123

which God has commanded Him to speak (verses 49, 50). To reject Christ and His teaching is to reject God (verse 48). To believe on Him is to receive One who has come as light into the world (verse 46).

In St. Paul's Cathedral and in the Chapel at Keble College, Oxford, there are two well-known and almost identical paintings by Holman Hunt. They show Jesus as the Light of the world. Part of John Ruskin's letter to *The Times* on 5 May 1854, describing the paintings, reads as follows: 'The legend beneath it (the painting) is the beautiful verse—"Behold I stand at the door and knock. If any man hear my voice and open the door, I will come in to him, and will sup with him, and he with me" (Rev. 3:20). On the left hand side of the picture is seen this door of the human soul. It is fast barred; its bars and nails are rusty; it is knitted and bound to its stanchions by creeping tendrils of ivy, showing that it has never been opened. . . . Christ approaches it in the night time . . .'

So Jesus Christ may approach us. If we believe that He is the Son of God and the Saviour of sinners, and if we are ready to receive Him as personal Saviour, Master and God, then we could open the door of our lives and ask Him to come in and abide with us for ever. Here is a prayer we could use.

'Lord Jesus, I admit I am a sinner, living a self-centred life, and I confess my sins to You, especially those on my conscience.
I believe that You are the Son of God and the Saviour of sinners and that You died for *my* sins on the cross, bearing the judgment I deserved.
I have counted the cost and I am willing to die to self and live for You, with Your help, and to serve You in the fellowship of Your church. So I come to You and receive You into my life as my Saviour, Master and God, now and for ever. Amen.'

Jesus said, 'Behold, I stand at the door and knock; if *any one* hears my voice and opens the door, *I will come in*' (see Revelation 3:20).

1 Now before the feast of the Passover, when Jesus knew that his hour had come to depart out of this world to the Father, having loved his own who were in the world, he loved them to the end. ²And during supper, when the devil had already put it into the heart of Judas Iscariot, Simon's son, to betray him, ³Jesus, knowing that the Father had given all things into his hands, and that he had come from God and was going to God, ⁴rose from supper, laid aside his garments, and girded himself with a towel. ⁵Then he poured water into a basin, and began to wash the disciples' feet, and to wipe them with the towel with which he was girded. ⁶He came to Simon Peter; and Peter said to him, 'Lord, do you wash my feet?' ⁷Jesus answered him, 'What I am doing you do not know now, but afterwards you will understand.' ⁸Peter said to him, 'You shall never wash my feet.' Jesus answered him, 'If I do not wash you, you have no part in me.' ⁹Simon Peter said to him, 'Lord, not my feet only but also my hands and my head!' ¹⁰Jesus said to him, 'He who has bathed does not need to wash, except for his feet, but he is clean all over; and you are clean, but not all of you.' ¹¹For he knew who was to betray him; that was why he said, 'You are not all clean.'

12 When he had washed their feet, and taken his garments, and resumed his place, he said to them, 'Do you know what I have done to you? ¹³You call me Teacher and Lord; and you are right, for so I am. ¹⁴If I then, your Lord and Teacher, have washed your feet, you also ought to wash one another's feet. ¹⁵For I have given you an example, that you also should do as I have done to you. ¹⁶Truly, truly, I say to you, a servant is not greater than his master; nor is he who is sent greater than he who sent him. ¹⁷If you know these things, blessed are you if you do them.'

The scene is the upper room in Jerusalem. The twelve disciples have met with Jesus to eat the Passover meal.* It is clear that a new

* See R. V. G. Tasker, *The Gospel according to St. John*, p. 153, where it is suggested that verse 1 of this chapter is the heading for the next five chapters and should be taken separately. In this way it does not imply that the Last Supper could not be the Passover meal.

stage in the ministry of Jesus has begun. His public ministry is over. Now He must concentrate on teaching and training the disciples to face up to the future.

John does not give us all the information about the Last Supper that can be found in the other Gospels. Presumably it would be well known to the early Christians. He does not mention the preparation of the room for the meal (Matthew 26:17–19; Mark 14:12–16; Luke 22:7–13) or the quarrelling of the disciples over rival claims to greatness (Matthew 20:25–28; Mark 10:42–45; Luke 22:24–27). There is no mention of the symbolic taking of bread and wine which is central in the other Gospels (Matthew 26:26–29; Mark 14:22–25; Luke 22:17–19). But He does recount another equally symbolic action.

In Palestine, the roads were often inches deep in dust in dry weather, and turned to liquid mud in wet weather. Normally therefore a slave would take water and a towel and wash the feet of the guests, whose sandals were not designed to keep out the dust. It seems that on this occasion no slave was available, and the disciples were more interested in arguing about the best seats in the kingdom than in doing the work of a slave. No-one volunteered. But during supper Jesus rose up, laid aside His garments, put on a slave's apron, and taking a basin and water began to wash the disciples' feet. In recording this symbolic action of Jesus, John emphasizes two things.

a. An example of humility (verses 1–5)

'*Jesus knew that his hour had come to depart out of this world to the Father*', yet He deliberately and symbolically illustrated by this action how He was laying aside His Father's glory. He became like a slave, and humbled Himself even to the death of the cross (see Philippians 2:5–11). Jesus knew that '*the Father had given all things into his hands*' (verse 3), yet later He was prepared to submit to the insignificant authority of the cruel and vacillating Pontius Pilate. Jesus knew that '*he had come from God and was going to God*' (verse 3), yet, although He was conscious of His own majesty and authority, He deliberately put on the apron of a slave, and washed the disciples' feet as a sign that, like the ideal servant of Old

126

Testament prophecy, He was willing to 'pour out his soul to death' (Isaiah 53:12).

b. A call for humility (verses 6–17)

It is not enough to *call* Jesus 'Teacher' and 'Lord'. It is not enough to admire His example of humility. He calls us to follow His example and 'to put on the apron of humility' (*cf.* 1 Peter 5:5). This story underlines two aspects of humility in particular.

1. *The humility of receiving* (verses 6–11). It is often a deeper mark of humility to receive something from a friend than to do something for him. Most of us, like Simon Peter, instinctively prefer to do something for God than to receive something from Him. 'Lord, do *you* wash *my* feet?' Jesus explains that Peter will not fully understand the significance of what He is doing until later, but insists, 'If *I* do not wash *you*, you have no part in me.' Peter then, true to form, blurts out impulsively, 'Lord, not my feet only but also my hands and my head!'

We can now understand what Jesus means. The washing of Peter's feet is symbolic of the cleansing from sin which Peter must receive from Christ, if he is to have fellowship with Him. Such initial cleansing, symbolized by baptism, symbolic of forgiveness and new life, is once and for all and cannot be repeated. But it must be humbly received from Christ Himself. Some commentators make much of the different Greek words used: 'He who has bathed (*louō*) does not need to wash (*niptō*), except for his feet, but he is clean all over.' A man normally bathed (*louō*) before he went out for a meal. When he reached the house where he would feast, he did not need to bathe again, but his feet would need to be washed (*niptō*) once more. It is certainly true that a Christian receives new life once he is washed and accepted by God. He is brought into a new relationship which cannot be altered. But he also needs daily to confess his sins and he needs daily forgiveness. He needs to have the dirt of each day washed away. For sin cannot break our relationship with Jesus Christ, but it can spoil our fellowship with Him. In a letter to Christians, John assures us that 'if we confess our sins, he is faithful and just, and will forgive our sins and cleanse us from all unrighteousness' (1 John 1:9).

2. *The humility of serving* (verses 12–17). 'If I then, your Lord and Teacher, have washed your feet, you also ought to wash one another's feet.' Jesus calls His disciples not only to receive His cleansing but to *serve* other people.

There are sections of the Christian church which still observe the ritual of feet-washing as carefully as the Lord's Supper and Baptism. But Jesus intends us to follow His example of humble service in our daily lives. We fail to see the force of what He is saying if we are not willing to do a menial task for His sake, if we stand on our dignity or insist on our rights. There are many opportunities for Christians today to exercise such menial service. The modern Welfare State, which cares so much for the material and physical needs of men, often cannot meet the needs of loneliness, fear and depression which afflict less fortunate members of society. One of the tasks of the Christian church is to help create a community where Christians love one another, care for one another, accept one another. This will sometimes mean that a Christian will help to redecorate the room of an elderly couple, or mend a fuse or help with the shopping. If Jesus could do the task of a slave and wash the disciples' feet, there is no task too menial for His disciple. 'If you know these things, happy are you if you do them.'

29 THE LOVE OF JESUS
13:18–35

18'I am not speaking of you all; I know whom I have chosen; it is that the scripture may be fulfilled, "He who ate my bread has lifted his heel against me." 19I tell you this now, before it takes place, that when it does take place you may believe that I am he. 20Truly, truly, I say to you, he who receives any one whom I send receives me; and he who receives me receives him who sent me.'

21 When Jesus had thus spoken, he was troubled in spirit,

and testified, 'Truly, truly, I say to you, one of you will betray me.' 22The disciples looked at one another, uncertain of whom he spoke. 23One of his disciples, whom Jesus loved, was lying close to the breast of Jesus; 24so Simon Peter beckoned to him and said, 'Tell us who it is of whom he speaks.' 25So lying thus, close to the breast of Jesus, he said to him, 'Lord, who is it?' 26Jesus answered, 'It is he to whom I shall give this morsel when I have dipped it.' So when he had dipped the morsel, he gave it to Judas, the son of Simon Iscariot. 27Then after the morsel, Satan entered into him. Jesus said to him, 'What you are going to do, do quickly.' 28Now no one at the table knew why he said this to him. 29Some thought that, because Judas had the money box, Jesus was telling him, 'Buy what we need for the feast'; or, that he should give something to the poor. 30So, after receiving the morsel, he immediately went out; and it was night.

31 When he had gone out, Jesus said, 'Now is the Son of man glorified, and in him God is glorified; 32if God is glorified in him, God will also glorify him in himself, and glorify him at once. 33Little children, yet a little while I am with you. You will seek me; and as I said to the Jews so now I say to you, "Where I am going you cannot come." 34A new commandment I give to you, that you love one another; even as I have loved you, that you also love one another. 35By this all men will know that you are my disciples, if you have love for one another.'

In the previous passage the humility of Jesus is contrasted with the pride of the disciples. Here the love of Jesus is contrasted with the treachery of Judas.

a. The treachery of Judas (verses 18–20)

Some writers have tried to whitewash the character of Judas, who is perhaps the most tragic figure in history. They have suggested that perhaps he was trying to force the hand of Jesus by this betrayal, in order that He might declare Himself to be the Messiah. But it is important to note all the evidence about Judas. In this Gospel, Judas is described as 'a devil' or 'adversary' (6:70, 71), as 'a thief' (12:4–6), as 'tempted by the devil' (13:2) and finally as possessed by Satan, for 'Satan entered into him' (13:27). The fact that the other disciples did not apparently suspect that Judas would betray Jesus (verses 27–29) shows that Judas must have been a clever hypocrite as well. When Jesus revealed that there was one of them who would betray Him, and that He knew who it would be, He emphasized the extent of his treachery by quoting the Old Testament scripture, 'He who ate my bread has lifted his heel against me.' A close friend would deal brutally with Him.

Jesus gave this information to the disciples so that later they would understand that Jesus had divine foreknowledge of the events that led to His death, and would be strengthened to acknowledge Him as God's Messiah (verse 19). At the same time He emphasizes the high calling of those who represent Christ in the world, so that they can understand that a man whose heart is not right could not remain with them (verse 20).

b. The love of Jesus (verses 21–35)

In spite of Judas' treachery Jesus loved him 'to the end'. John records that Jesus 'was troubled in spirit' (verse 21). He was in great distress at the enormity of Judas's betrayal. Yet He continued to love him. It is probable that Judas sat on the left of Jesus at supper, as it appears that Jesus could carry on a conversation with him without moving from His place. Simon Peter had to beckon to John when he wanted to put a question to Jesus, so he could not have been in that position. John was clearly on the right of Jesus (verse 25). If Judas did sit on the left of Jesus he was of course sitting in the place of highest honour, usually kept for the host's intimate friend. The 'morsel' was probably a choice piece of the dish, and was offered to Judas as an expression of special friendship (verse 26).*

Judas's rejection of this final appeal by Jesus is the moment when Satan and darkness fill his soul. There comes a time when the love of Jesus is so often rejected that He has to leave us to settle our own destiny. Jesus says, 'What you are going to do, do quickly.' It was night: not only in the streets of Jerusalem but also in the soul of Judas.

The factors involved in man's choice or rejection of Jesus Christ

* It is also believed to have been common practice for the 'morsel' to be used when two people were making a bargain. Rather than shaking hands or signing a contract, a morsel dipped in wine was given and received and this pledge was absolutely binding on both parties. So Judas took the morsel knowing full well that he would be breaking a contract with Jesus.

are not simple ones. Nor is it possible for the finite mind of man to understand perfectly the relationship between God's plan and man's responsibility. The narrative has made plain that Jesus loved Judas to the end, and that Judas was responsible for his own actions. Yet when Judas had finally rejected Christ's appeal of love, Jesus could say, 'Now is the Son of man glorified, and in him God is glorified.' God was going to overrule the wickedness and treachery of men in accordance with His own plan and foreknowledge (see Acts 2:23). The death of Christ was to be the moment of glory to be followed by the victory of the resurrection and ascension (verse 32). The disciples could not yet share in that glory (verse 33), but they could glorify God by loving one another in the same kind of selfless, humble, patient and sacrificial way that Jesus loved them. This was to be the badge of their discipleship whereby people would know they belonged to Jesus Christ (verses 34, 35).

Modern man often feels he is part of a machine, that life is absurd or pre-determined, that there is no loving or logical purpose at all. As a result he often blames his environment or even his hormones for his own predicament. Arthur Koestler actually suggests that if man is to be prevented from blowing himself up, he may have to receive injections of some synthetic hormones to change his character. In Sartre's novels the same pessimistic view of man is depicted, and someone has called Sartre's world a 'world without grace'. The story of Judas reminds us, however, that man is responsible for his actions, and that the world is not without grace or a loving purpose. But when grace and love are persistently spurned then man, like Judas, 'goes to his own place' and settles his own destiny.

36 Simon Peter said to him, 'Lord, where are you going?' Jesus answered, 'Where I am going you cannot follow me now; but you shall follow afterward.' [37]Peter said to him, 'Lord, why cannot I follow you now? I will lay down my life for you.' [38]Jesus answered, 'Will you lay down your life for me? Truly, truly, I say to you, the cock will not crow, till you have denied me three times.

1 'Let not your hearts be troubled; believe in God, believe also in me. [2]In my Father's house are many rooms; if it were not so, would I have told you that I go to prepare a place for you? [3]And when I go and prepare a place for you, I will come again and will take you to myself, that where I am you may be also. [4]And you know the way where I am going.' [5]Thomas said to him, 'Lord, we do not know where you are going; how can we know the way?' [6]Jesus said to him, 'I am the way, and the truth, and the life; no one comes to the Father, but by me. [7]If you had known me, you would have known my Father also; henceforth you know him and have seen him.'

8 Philip said to him, 'Lord, show us the Father, and we shall be satisfied.' [9]Jesus said to him, 'Have I been with you so long, and yet you do not know me, Philip? He who has seen me has seen the Father; how can you say, "Show us the Father"? [10]Do you not believe that I am in the Father and the Father in me? The words that I say to you I do not speak on my own authority; but the Father who dwells in me does his works. [11]Believe me that I am in the Father and the Father in me; or else believe me for the sake of the works themselves.'

Judas had gone. Jesus was soon to go where they could not come. Perplexed and no doubt a little afraid, the disciples began to question Jesus. The three questions that are recorded in this passage all raise important and relevant issues. Simon Peter asks the first question.

a. 'Lord, where are you going?' (13:36–14:4)

Was it to die? Then Simon Peter wanted to die too. 'Lord, why cannot I follow you now? I will lay down my life for you.' These were brave words and typical of the warm-hearted, impulsive Peter. But they promised more than they achieved. As Jesus pointed out, for all his self-confidence, Simon Peter would in fact deny that he ever knew Jesus. Jesus knew Peter through and through. But it is typical of His graciousness that, although He knew how weak Peter was, He saw in him nonetheless the stuff that martyrs are made of. 'Where I am going you cannot follow me now; but you shall follow afterward' (*cf.* John 21:18, 19).

Jesus then turns to all the disciples (verses 1–4) and answers Peter's question. He is going to His Father's house (heaven) to prepare a place for His disciples. He then promises to come again to receive them and welcome them and be with them for ever.

Heaven is where Jesus is. It is a place of rest. It is a place prepared for those who have trusted in Jesus Christ. When Jesus says, 'Believe in God, believe also in me', He is encouraging the disciples to turn their thoughts from fears of the immediate future on earth to thoughts of their ultimate destiny in heaven. It is such confidence that enables Christians to keep present anxieties in perspective, just as the apostle Paul was able to write later, 'I consider that the sufferings of this present time are not worth comparing with the glory that is to be revealed to us' (Romans 8:18). Bertrand Russell* once wrote: 'The belief that we survive death seems to me . . . to have no scientific basis. I do not think it would ever have arisen except as an emotional reaction to the fear of death.' Professor Hoyle† wrote: 'While our intelligences are powerful enough to penetrate deeply into the evolution of this quite incredible universe, we still have not the smallest clue to our own fate.' In contrast to these Jesus said, 'Let not your hearts be troubled; believe in God, believe also in me. In my Father's house are many rooms; if it were not so, would I have told you that I go to prepare a place for you?'

Jesus concludes: 'You know the way where I am going.' At

* From an article in *The Times* later published in a book containing a series of articles entitled *The Great Mystery of Life Hereafter*.

† F. Hoyle, *The Nature of the Universe*.

133

this Thomas, somewhat sceptical and pessimistic, interrupts with another question.

b. 'Lord, we do not know where you are going: how can we know the way?' (verses 5-7)

How can anyone know the way who does not know the destination? We must be grateful to Thomas for pressing the point. It is a solemn and sad thing to be unsure of our future destiny. Jesus' answer is both simple and profound. 'I am the way, and the truth, and the life.' The way to heaven is through Jesus Himself. Man has often made the way to God and to heaven complicated and difficult. Many directions are given, often to our bewilderment. Truths and propositions are presented to us in difficult theological language. Taboos and prohibitions sometimes make the way unwelcome. But Jesus cuts through all this. *He* is the way to God. If you asked a man in the East to show you the way to a certain place, he might well say 'I am the way', by which he would mean, 'Follow me and I will bring you to your destination.' Jesus makes this claim concerning man's ultimate destiny. He claims, moreover, that He is the *only* way to the Father, that He alone embodies truth, and that He alone is the source of eternal life. When a man is introduced to Jesus Christ, he is introduced to God. Jesus is the way to the Father, the full truth about the Father, the very life of the Father. Other systems and philosophies have tried to bridge the gap between man and God. Jesus *is* the bridge between man and God.

Now it is Philip's turn to ask a question.

c. 'Lord, show us the Father, and we shall be satisfied' (verses 8-11)

Philip was a practical man who did not understand theological or mystical language. He would be satisfied if he could see God with his own eyes as clearly as he could see Jesus. Jesus gently rebukes him for not understanding and then says, 'He who has seen me has seen the Father.'

There was a day when death had darkened the home of the Scottish author, Thomas Carlyle. Someone, taking a New Testament, opened it at the Gospel of John and read the familiar words, 'Let not your heart be troubled . . . In my Father's house are many mansions.' 'Aye,' muttered the bereaved man. 'If you were God you had a right to say that, but if you were only a man, what do you know any more than the rest of us?' Carlyle's query is answered in these words, 'He who has seen me has seen the Father.' The evidence that Jesus gives to substantiate this claim is threefold.

1. *His personality* (verse 10). Surely the intimate relationship between Jesus and His Father must have been apparent to the disciples. He always did those things that pleased the Father (see John 8:29).

2. *His words*. No-one ever spoke like Jesus (John 7:46). 'He whom God has sent utters the words of God' (3:34).

3. *His works*. His miracles and mighty deeds all authenticated His message and His claims. No-one could do the things that Jesus did unless He was God.

31 A NEW RELATIONSHIP
14:12–17

12 'Truly, truly, I say to you, he who believes in me will also do the works that I do; and greater works than these will he do, because I go to the Father. 13Whatever you ask in my name, I will do it, that the Father may be glorified in the Son; 14if you ask anything in my name, I will do it.

15 'If you love me, you will keep my commandments. 16And I will pray the Father, and he will give you another Counsellor, to be with you for ever, 17even the Spirit of truth, whom the world cannot receive, because it neither sees him nor knows him; you know him, for he dwells with you, and will be in you.'

'Does it work?' That is what many people ask about Christianity. Jesus now outlines to the disciples some of the exciting privileges and responsibilities that follow personal commitment to Him.

a. A new relationship (verses 12–14)

They will experience this when He leaves them and returns to His Father in heaven. The privileges of this relationship will be so great that they should be rejoicing at the prospect of His leaving them (see verse 28). 'For the Father is greater than I.' Jesus here acknowledges both the limitations and the voluntary subordination of His earthly ministry in relation to His heavenly Father. But once He has returned to share once again the glory of His Father, the resources available to the disciples will be limitless.

b. A new power in prayer (verses 12, 13)

Once Jesus has ascended, His ministry will no longer be confined to Palestine. Through the power of prayer the believer will see greater works done in the name of Jesus than in His earthly ministry. These works will be greater in the sense that they will not be confined to one place at a time. Greater also because the full experience of the new birth and the knowledge of God in Jesus was possible only after the death, resurrection and ascension of Jesus. The secret of power is prayer *'in the name of Jesus'*. This must mean prayer in accordance with His will (no man will lend his name for a cause that is contrary to his own purposes and wishes). It must also mean prayer 'counting on the authority and power of Jesus'— as a man may use the name of an influential friend to gain access into normally inaccessible places. It also clearly means prayer that is concerned not with selfish desires but with the glory of God. The practical apostle James once wrote: 'You do not have, because you do not ask. You ask and do not receive, because you ask wrongly, to spend it on your passions' (James 4:2, 3). The great cricketer and missionary, C. T. Studd, at the end of his resources in China, proved the power of prayer. 'My family in England knew nothing of our circumstances,' he wrote. 'The last of our supplies was finished. The mail came once a fortnight. If the postman brought no relief, starvation stared us in the face.' So C. T. Studd and his wife prayed to God in the name of Jesus. The mail arrived. The last letter was from a stranger, Frank Crossley. It said this: 'I have for some reason received the command of God to send you £100. I have never met you. I have only heard of you, and that not often, but God has prevented me from sleeping tonight by this command. Why He should command me to send you this, you will know better than I.'* There is power in prayer.

c. A new strength to obey (verses 15–17)

'If you love me, you will keep my commandments.' The teaching of the new moralists suggests that love removes the necessity for law. 'Nothing can of itself always be labelled as "wrong". One cannot, for instance, start from the position "sex relations before marriage" or "divorce" are wrong or sinful in themselves. They may be in 99 cases or even 100 out of 100, but they are not intrinsically so, for the only intrinsic evil is lack of love.'† Jesus contradicts this view of law: love is blind without the law. Love for Christ will be demonstrated by obedience to the law. The new element in Christ's teaching is that the disciple of Christ will discover that he *wants* to keep God's law and that he will have *power* to do so. This is because, in fulfilment of Old Testament promises that God would write His law on our hearts and take away the heart of stone (Jeremiah 31:33; Ezekiel 36:26), Jesus promises that He will come and dwell in our hearts by His Spirit, so that we may have both the power and the desire to keep His commandments.

Who is the 'Spirit of truth'? (verse 17). He is described as *'another* Counsellor'. The Greek word (*allon*) means 'another of the same kind as'. He is not a vague influence or power. He is *divine* like Jesus, yet a different person.‡ Indeed Jesus can speak of Him interchangeably with Himself and with His Father. Jesus tells us in this passage that the Counsellor will dwell with us and in us (verse 17). At the same time He says that He Himself will come to the disciples and dwell in them (verse 20). Later He says that the Father would come and make His home in the lives and personalities of His followers. In the New Testament letters we find the same kind of language. The early Christians could speak of God dwelling in them (1 Corinthians 3:16), Christ dwelling in them

* Norman P. Grubb, *C. T. Studd: Cricketer and Pioneer*, pp. 98, 99.
† J. A. T. Robinson, *Honest to God*, p. 118.
‡ See R. V. G. Tasker, *The Gospel according to St. John*, p. 172.

(Colossians 1:27) and the Spirit possessing their lives (Romans 8:14–16). The doctrine of the Trinity (God as three persons in one) was never formally worked out in the New Testament; but it was implicit in the teaching of Jesus, and inevitably arose out of the experience of the early Christians. The disciples believed in one God. Yet they were compelled by the evidence to believe that God became man in Jesus, and that Jesus continued with them in the power of the indwelling Spirit. In Christian experience it is not difficult to believe in one God in three persons. The unity of God is not a mathematical unity, any more than the unity of the atom. There is such a thing as organic unity.

He is *personal*, too, for Jesus speaks of Him as 'teaching' and 'reminding' (verse 26). Jesus also calls the Spirit *'Counsellor'* (*paraklētos*), which literally means 'someone called alongside to help'. Sometimes the Greeks used this word to describe an advocate in a court of law, or an expert called in to advise, or even someone called in to raise the morale of dispirited soldiers. As Dr. Leon Morris has said, 'the significance of the word is not so much "there, there, little one!" as "up guards and at 'em!" It is not soothing syrup but a clarion call.' It is the Spirit who gives us strength to obey God.

32 A NEW ASSURANCE
14:18–31

18 'I will not leave you desolate; I will come to you. ¹⁹Yet a little while, and the world will see me no more, but you will see me; because I live, you will live also. ²⁰In that day you will know that I am in my Father, and you in me, and I in you. ²¹He who has my commandments and keeps them, he it is who loves me; and he who loves me will be loved by my Father, and I will love him and manifest myself to him.' ²²Judas (not Iscariot) said to him, 'Lord, how is it that you will manifest yourself to us, and not to the world?' ²³Jesus answered him, 'If a man loves me, he will keep my word, and my Father will love

him, and we will come to him and make our home with him. 24He who does not love me does not keep my words; and the word which you hear is not mine but the Father's who sent me.

25 'These things I have spoken to you, while I am still with you. 26But the Counsellor, the Holy Spirit, whom the Father will send in my name, he will teach you all things, and bring to your remembrance all that I have said to you. 27Peace I leave with you; my peace I give to you; not as the world gives do I give to you. Let not your hearts be troubled, neither let them be afraid. 28You heard me say to you, "I go away, and I will come to you." If you loved me, you would have rejoiced, because I go to the Father; for the Father is greater than I. 29And now I have told you before it takes place, so that when it does take place, you may believe. 30I will no longer talk much with you, for the ruler of this world is coming. He has no power over me; 31but I do as the Father has commanded me, so that the world may know that I love the Father. Rise, let us go hence.'

Once the Spirit has made His home in the personality of the believer, he experiences life and the assurance that Christ lives in him (verses 18–20). Jesus promises the disciples that He will not leave them desolate (or like orphans) (verse 18) but that the Spirit will enable them to know that they belong to God.

There is an old Arab proverb that says:

'He that knows not, and knows not that he knows not, is a fool— *shun him*.

He that knows not, and knows that he knows not, is simple— *teach him*.

He that knows, and knows not that he knows, is asleep—*wake him*.

He that knows, and knows that he knows, is a wise man— *follow him*.'

Jesus promised the Spirit to the disciples, that they might *know* that they possessed life in Him. The Spirit will give them certainty through inner conviction, the Word of God and the peace of God.

a. Inner conviction (verse 20)

'In that day you will *know* that I am in my Father, and you in me, and I in you.'

139

b. The Word of God (verses 21–26)

Jesus calls the Counsellor the Spirit of *truth* (verse 17). He is given to teach the disciples all things, and bring to their remembrance all that Jesus had said to them (verse 26). What Jesus said, God said (verse 24). This is the basis of the Christian belief that the New Testament writers as well as the Old were 'inspired by God' as they wrote. The apostle Paul claimed: 'We have received not the spirit of the world, but the Spirit which is from God, that we might understand the gifts bestowed on us by God. And we impart this in words not taught by human wisdom but taught by the Spirit, interpreting spiritual truths to those who possess the Spirit' (1 Corinthians 2:12, 13).

Jesus teaches in this passage that it is in keeping God's Word (that is, what we call the Old and New Testaments) that God makes Himself known to the believer. This is His answer to Judas's question, 'How is it that you will manifest yourself to us, and not to the world?' We show our love to God by reading, receiving and obeying God's Word. He shows His love to us in revealing Himself to us as we read, by the work of the Holy Spirit (see verses 21–26). If the Bible is coming alive to us, this is an assurance that God is with us. If we neglect to read the Bible or disobey its commands, then we prove that we do not love God (verse 24).

In his fascinating book, *Miracle on the River Kwai*, Ernest Gordon tells of the way in which the reading of the Gospels came alive to desperate men in a prisoner-of-war camp. They searched the New Testament to find whether Jesus was real and relevant to them in their situation. 'Through our readings and discussions we gradually came to *know Jesus*. He was one of us. He would understand our problems because they were the kind of problems He had faced Himself . . . As we read and talked He became flesh and blood . . . What He was, what He did, what He said all made sense to us.'

c. The peace of God (verses 27–31)

Whatever the circumstances the disciples would be given the assurance of God's presence by the gift of peace. This too would be a fruit of the Spirit, which would become theirs after Jesus had returned to His Father. Satan, or the ruler of this world, may be powerful; but he has no power over Jesus (verse 30). He might do all he could to divert Jesus from His path to the cross. But Jesus Christ knew that peace is to be found in loving God and doing His will whatever it costs (verse 31).

On 23 January 1964 Pastor Yona Kanamuzayi was martyred in the Ruanda riots. He was carried off from his home, shot in the back and then pushed into the river. Before he died he prayed for his executioners, and then, according to an eyewitness, went to his death joyfully singing a hymn. The soldiers were all amazed. They had never before seen a man walking calmly and unafraid to meet his murderers as he did, 'like a man just taking a stroll'.* But when Jesus said to the disciples, 'Peace I leave with you; my peace I give to you', He meant it to be true for all believers, whatever the circumstances. When He said to the disciples 'Rise, let *us* go hence', He made it clear that future crises and difficulties would be faced together with Him.

33 A NEW COMMUNITY
15:1–17

1 'I am the true vine, and my Father is the vine-dresser. ²Every branch of mine that bears no fruit, he takes away, and every branch that does bear fruit he prunes, that it may bear more fruit. ³You are already made clean by the word which I have spoken to you. ⁴Abide in me, and I in you. As the branch cannot bear fruit by itself, unless it abides in the vine, neither can you, unless you abide in me. ⁵I am the vine, you are the branches. He who abides in me, and I in him, he it is that bears much fruit, for apart from me you can do nothing. ⁶If a man does not abide in me, he is cast forth as a branch and withers; and the branches are gathered, thrown into the fire and burned. ⁷If you abide in me, and my words abide in you, ask whatever you will, and it

* J. E. Church, *Forgive them*, p. 15.

141

shall be done for you. [8]By this my Father is glorified, that you bear much fruit, and so prove to be my disciples. [9]As the Father has loved me, so have I loved you; abide in my love. [10]If you keep my commandments, you will abide in my love, just as I have kept my Father's commandments and abide in his love. [11]These things I have spoken to you, that my joy may be in you, and that your joy may be full.

12 'This is my commandment, that you love one another as I have loved you. [13]Greater love has no man than this, that a man lay down his life for his friends. [14]You are my friends if you do what I command you. [15]No longer do I call you servants, for the servant does not know what his master is doing; but I have called you friends, for all that I have heard from my Father I have made known to you. [16]You did not choose me, but I chose you and appointed you that you should go and bear fruit and that your fruit should abide; so that whatever you ask the Father in my name, he may give it to you. [17]This I command you, to love one another.'

John Wesley used to quote the words, 'There is no such thing as solitary religion.' Today there is a certain amount of disenchantment with the church and 'organized religion', so that Wesley's view is sometimes ignored.

I have often heard it said, as a result, 'Surely I don't have to go to church to be a Christian?' or, 'I can be a Christian, even a good Christian, without going to church.'

In this chapter Jesus makes it clear that it is God's purpose to do His work in the world through His people, not only as individuals, but as members of a divine community—as branches in a vine. If we belong to Christ, as one branch sharing the very sap or life of the Vine, then we also belong to His church. There are other branches in the Vine, even as there are many members of a body (to use Paul's metaphor for the church), or stones in a building, or members of a family, or citizens of a kingdom. God's purpose is that once we belong to Him, we belong to His people.

In the Old Testament the vine was often used as a picture of God's relationship to His people. God planted the vine, and cared for it. Israel was the vine itself. Sadly, Israel failed in many ways to fulfil God's purposes (Isaiah 5:1–7). She was described as a 'degenerate' vine (Jeremiah 2:21) or 'empty vine' (Hosea 10:1, AV). In Jesus, however, the people of God will fulfil God's purposes. 'I am the *true* vine,' said Jesus. Fruitfulness of life and character (*cf.* Galatians 5:22, 23) and effective service and prayer (verse 16) are part of God's purpose for His people. They depend on '*abiding*' in Jesus, in fellowship with other believers. To abide in Christ means at least four things for the individual and the church.

a. To be united to Christ

A Christian is not only someone who believes certain facts about Christ, or who follows the Christian ethic. He is someone as vitally in touch with Christ by faith as a fruit-bearing branch is vitally in touch with the vine. As the branch shares the sap, the life of the vine, and so bears fruit, so the Christian, united by faith to Christ, shares His life. He produces the fruit of the Spirit—love, joy, peace, patience, kindness, goodness, faithfulness, gentleness, self-control (Galatians 5:22, 23).

The tragedy of Judas is that, although he associated with the disciples and with Jesus, he was like a branch apparently attached to the vine, but in fact dead and fruitless. So he did not really share in the 'life' of Christ. He was not 'clean' (verse 3) like the other disciples. He had not believed in Christ in his heart, or obeyed Him in his life. So, tragically, he was cast forth as a dead branch and withered. When vine wood is dead it is useless for anything but burning. A dead, nominal Christian, even though he may be a church member or office-bearer, is as useless in the service of God as a dead branch. He must likewise expect the judgment of God unless he is cleansed and united by faith to Christ.

b. To be dependent on Christ

To abide in Christ is to depend on Christ (verses 4, 5). 'Apart from me you can do nothing.' How do we learn daily dependence upon Jesus Christ? The clearest answer is in verse 7: 'If you abide in me, and my words abide in you, ask whatever you will, and it shall be done for you.' In the same way that we need daily bread to sustain us physically, so we need spiritual food, the words of Jesus and of the Bible, to sustain us spiritually. For as Jesus Himself quoted, 'Man shall not live by bread alone, but by every word that proceeds from the mouth of God' (Matthew 4:4). Jesus goes on to say that if His words take root in our lives by daily meditation upon them, and by daily obedience, we shall also learn dependence on Him through prayer. When we are dependent upon Christ our prayers become more confident (verse 7) and our lives become more Christlike (note 'much fruit' in verse 8). In this way we bring glory to God and demonstrate the genuineness of our own discipleship (verse 8).

There is one other way that God teaches us dependence upon Jesus. 'Every branch that does bear fruit he *prunes*, that it may bear more fruit.' There is dead wood, sins of pride, independence, selfishness, impatience, covetousness and so on, that needs to be cut away from our lives if we are to become more Christlike. So God's word to us is sometimes like a pruning-knife. It hurts, it rebukes us, it humbles us. Sometimes He speaks to us through the circumstances of our lives, and chastens and humbles us through suffering, disappointment, or bereavement. If He does it is *always* for our good—that we might be more Christlike. The divine Gardener is a God of love.

c. To be obedient to Christ

To abide in Christ involves *obedience*. It is not enough to believe—and then to sit back for 'God to do it all'. Jesus commands us to 'abide in my love' in response to His great love for us (verse 9). Indeed we can abide in His love only as we keep His commandments. The Christian is not saved by keeping God's law—for he cannot perfectly fulfil the demands of God's law. Only Jesus Christ has done that. But once the Christian has been saved from the guilt and judgment he deserves by the free and undeserved love of God in Christ, he responds to that love by keeping God's law. That is the way he shows his love to Christ. That is also the only way to discover the joy that Jesus gives (verse 11).

Jesus commands us not only to love Him, but also to *love one another* (verse 12). Here again, He does not ask from us slavish obedience, or make unreasonable demands. Jesus' love for us was such that He gave His life for us. He gave His life that we might become His friends. He reveals His Father's secrets to His friends as they obey Him. He chose us to be His friends that we might go into the world to be effective (fruitful) in our lives and witness. All the strength, love, patience, endurance and tolerance needed to love one another can be ours as we ask God to give this to us in the name of Jesus. I once asked a young woman, who had left a good secretarial job in this country to serve God overseas, to tell me the difference Jesus Christ had made to her life since she personally began to follow Him. She said: 'I found that God gave me the power to love those I would not normally like.' When certain pagans in the first century said 'See how these Christians love one another', it was a tribute to the life and love of Jesus in the personalities of Christian disciples, as they obeyed His command to 'abide in his love'.

d. To continue with Christ

To abide in Christ means to continue in dependence and obedience all our lives. The word literally means 'to remain'. It is not enough to begin with Christ, we must *continue* with Him. Jesus said elsewhere, 'He who endures to the end will be saved' (Matthew 10:22). Paul, putting it from God's point of view, said, 'I am sure that he who began a good work in you will bring it to completion at the day of Jesus Christ' (Philippians 1:6). We must 'work out (our) own salvation with fear and trembling; for God is at work in (us), both to will and to work for his good pleasure' (Philippians 2:12, 13). As we continue to trust and obey, so His life and power will sustain us to the end, and so we prove to be His disciples indeed.

To read the Bible, to pray and to have fellowship with other Christians is far more than a religious duty. It is the God-appointed way to trust and obey the risen Lord and to receive His life and grace and power for effective Christ-like living.

18 'If the world hates you, know that it has hated me before it hated you. 19If you were of the world, the world would love its own; but because you are not of the world, but I chose you out of the world, therefore the world hates you. 20Remember the word that I said to you, "A servant is not greater than his master." If they persecuted me, they will persecute you; if they kept my word, they will keep yours also. 21But all this they will do to you on my account, because they do not know him who sent me. 22If I had not come and spoken to them, they would not have sin; but now they have no excuse for their sin. 23He who hates me hates my Father also. 24If I had not done among them the works which no one else did, they would not have sin; but now they have seen and hated both me and my Father. 25It is to fulfil the word that is written in their law, "They hated me without a cause." 26But when the Counsellor comes, whom I shall send to you from the Father, even the Spirit of truth, who proceeds from the Father, he will bear witness to me; 27and you also are witnesses, because you have been with me from the beginning.

1 'I have said all this to you to keep you from falling away. 2They will put you out of the synagogues; indeed, the hour is coming when whoever kills you will think he is offering service to God. 3And they will do this because they have not known the Father, nor me. 4But I have said these things to you, that when their hour comes you may remember that I told you of them.

'I did not say these things to you from the beginning, because I was with you. 5But now I am going to him who sent me; yet none of you asks me, "Where are you going?" 6But because I have said these things to you, sorrow has filled your hearts. 7Nevertheless I tell you the truth: it is to your advantage that I go away, for if I do not go away, the Counsellor will not come to you; but if I go I will send him to you. 8And when he comes, he will convince the world of sin and of righteousness and of judgment: 9of sin, because they do not believe in me; 10of righteousness, because I go to the Father, and you will see

me no more; "of judgment, because the ruler of this world is judged.'

Archbishop Temple once said that 'the Church of Jesus Christ is the only society that exists for the benefit of its non-members'. Christian fellowship is important. But so is Christian witness. Jesus has called and chosen His church 'to *go* and bear fruit' in the world. As Jesus taught elsewhere, His disciples are called to be *salt* in society (Matthew 5:13). Salt was rubbed into meat to prevent it from going bad. They were to be *light*, so that men would see their good works and glory their Father in heaven (Matthew 5:16).

Here Jesus reminds the disciples of the difficulties and dangers of witnessing for Him in a hostile world. A *witness* is someone who gives evidence of what he knows and has seen. 'You also are witnesses,' said Jesus to the disciples, 'because you have been with me from the beginning.' We also ought to be witnesses to Jesus Christ by our lives, by our actions, and by our words. This passage reminds us of two important facts that we need to bear in mind as we witness for Christ in the world.

a. The strength of the opposition

When John speaks about 'the world' he does not refer to the physical universe which God has created. He speaks of 'society organized without reference to God'. He speaks of the hearts and minds of men which are still controlled by the 'ruler of this world' (John 14:30), who is elsewhere called Satan, or 'the adversary'. Jesus did not think of Satan as an impersonal force, but as a personal adversary. '*He* has no power over me' (John 14:31). A Christian is someone who has handed over his life to the control of Jesus Christ, so he no longer belongs to 'the world' in the sense that we have defined the term (verse 19). Jesus Christ has chosen us 'out of the world' and freed us from its grip and its anti-Christian pressures. Now this brings us in conflict with society, even as it brought Jesus into conflict with the society of His own day. So the Christian may well face the hatred of the world, as Jesus did (verses 18, 19). He may well suffer persecution for his loyalty to the teaching of Jesus, for the words of Jesus expose man's lack of knowledge of God, and his rebellion against God (verses 21–23), and his refusal to accept the evidence of the life and works of Jesus. A minister friend of mine was talking for hours to an argumentative student who would not accept the message that my friend was explaining to him. The student rejected the message repeatedly. At last the minister said, 'It is time to go now: but I hope you realize that it is not me you are fighting against, but God.' The student's face suddenly changed. 'I'd never thought of it like that before', he said.

There is no real cause to hate Christ and His words (verse 25). But men in their stubbornness and pride will sometimes do so, and in doing so will hate and persecute His followers too. 'Remember the word that I said to you, "A servant is not greater than his master."'

In some parts of the world today men suffer physically for their loyalty to Christ.* For many of us, however, persecution may come with a raised eyebrow, a sneer, a supercilious smile, a taunt about 'religious mania', a deliberate cold-shouldering by some of our friends, a quite irrational outburst of annoyance from our parents or even from a minister of religion. The disciple of Jesus Christ should never underestimate the strength of the opposition.

b. The power of the Spirit (15:26–16:11)

'*But* when the Counsellor comes . . .' (verse 26). Yet again the disciples are reminded of the resources of God to help them face and overcome the opposition of the world. Jesus could say that the ruler of this world has no *power* over Him (14:31). The Christian can say that 'he who is in (us) is greater than he who is in the world' (1 John 4:4). The Counsellor bears witness to the truth through the disciples' witness to Christ. He will keep them from falling away under persecution by reminding them of Jesus' words (verses 3, 4). Indeed, Jesus' own departure to His Father will be an advantage to the disciples, because the Counsellor can do His work through them only after Jesus' death, resurrection and ascension.

What is the work that the Holy Spirit will do? The Greek word

* See, *e.g.*, Pastor Richard Wurmbrand, *Tortured for Christ*.

for 'to convince' (verse 8) that John uses means both to *convict*—
that is, to show that something is wrong—as well as to *convince*—
that is, to demonstrate the truth of something. The weakness of our
witness in the world lies precisely along these lines. We fail to convince people of their need of Christ, and we fail to convince them
of the truth about Christ. The Holy Spirit is given to God's people
to do precisely these two things.

We notice too that man's greatest 'sin' is to fail to believe in
Jesus (verse 9). The Holy Spirit alone can show men the seriousness of unbelief. The world needs to be convinced also that the
death of Jesus was not the end nor the failure of His mission
(verse 10). It was in fact the righteous act of a loving God, who
thereby is able to declare sinners 'righteous', 'accepted' or 'in the
right', because of Christ's death for sin on the cross. Finally, the
world needs to see that by Christ's death Satan is judged and
defeated and will eventually be destroyed (verse 11). How will men
today believe such astonishing truths? Jesus encourages the disciples to believe that when the Spirit comes upon them, He will
both convict and convince the unbeliever. There is a great deal of
evidence that the Spirit does the same work today through the
witness of ordinary Christians.

35 JESUS ENCOURAGES THE DISCIPLES
16:12–33

12 'I have yet many things to say to you, but you cannot bear
them now. ¹³When the Spirit of truth comes, he will guide you
into all the truth; for he will not speak on his own authority,
but whatever he hears he will speak, and he will declare to
you the things that are to come. ¹⁴He will glorify me, for he will
take what is mine and declare it to you. ¹⁵All that the Father
has is mine; therefore I said that he will take what is mine and
declare it to you.

16 'A little while, and you will see me no more; again a little while, and you will see me.' ¹⁷Some of his disciples said to one another, 'What is this that he says to us, "A little while, and you will not see me, and again a little while and you will see me"; and, "because I go to the Father"?' ¹⁸They said, 'What does he mean by "a little while"? We do not know what he means.' ¹⁹Jesus knew that they wanted to ask him; so he said to them, 'Is this what you are asking yourselves, what I meant by saying, "A little while, and you will not see me, and again a little while, and you will see me"? ²⁰Truly, truly, I say to you, you will weep and lament, but the world will rejoice; you will be sorrowful, but your sorrow will turn into joy. ²¹When a woman is in travail she has sorrow, because her hour has come; but when she is delivered of the child, she no longer remembers the anguish, for joy that a child is born into the world. ²²So you have sorrow now, but I will see you again and your hearts will rejoice, and no one will take your joy from you. ²³In that day you will ask me no questions. Truly, truly, I say to you, if you ask anything of the Father, he will give it to you in my name. ²⁴Hitherto you have asked nothing in my name; ask, and you will receive, that your joy may be full.

25 'I have said this to you in figures; the hour is coming when I shall no longer speak to you in figures but tell you plainly of the Father. ²⁶In that day you will ask in my name; and I do not say to you that I shall pray the Father for you; ²⁷for the Father himself loves you, because you have loved me and have believed that I came from the Father. ²⁸I came from the Father and have come into the world; again, I am leaving the world and going to the Father.'

29 His disciples said, 'Ah, now you are speaking plainly, not in any figure! ³⁰Now we know that you know all things, and need none to question you; by this we believe that you came from God.' ³¹Jesus answered them, 'Do you now believe? ³²The hour is coming, indeed it has come, when you will be scattered, every man to his home, and will leave me alone; yet I am not alone, for the Father is with me. ³³I have said this to you, that in me you may have peace. In the world you have tribulation; but be of good cheer, I have overcome the world.'

Jesus now gives specific encouragement to the eleven disciples, to prepare them for the crisis of the next few hours and days. He acknowledges that there are some things that He cannot say to them, for they would not be able to understand (verse 12). It is good for all of us to recognize that there are some truths and doctrines which we cannot fully understand until we know more about Christ and His purposes. We ought to want to go on from milk to meat in Christian teaching; but meat is indigestible for tiny babies. However, Jesus promises certain things for the future.

a. The guidance of the Spirit of truth (verses 12–15)

Here is another assurance to the Christian church that Jesus Christ foresaw the importance of leaving a record of the events and teaching of His life marked with the authority of God. So He promises the Spirit of truth to the disciples to lead them into truth, to reveal the things of God to them and to make Jesus real to them (see 14:25, 26). Elsewhere in the Gospels Jesus assumes the authority of the Old Testament. What the Scripture said, God said (compare Genesis 2:24 with Matthew 19:4–6).

Here He promises to the disciples, and later promises to Paul (compare Galatians 1:11–17 with 1 Corinthians 2:12, 13), that His Spirit would guide their writing and inspire their words.

The corollary for us is that we should approach the whole Bible humbly as revealing the truth of God, and ask for the guidance of God the Holy Spirit in seeking to understand and interpret it. A sun-dial is a useless object while the clouds obscure the sun. Once the sun shines on it, it fulfils its purpose. So the reading of the Bible can be a pointless exercise without the illumination of the Spirit of truth.

b. The joy of a personal relationship (verses 16–28)

When Jesus spoke about leaving the disciples, they naturally thought that their personal relationship with Him would be broken and lost for ever. In saying that in 'a little while' they would see Him no more, He obviously referred to His impending death. What did He mean, then, when He said, 'again a little while, and you will see me' and 'because I go to the Father'? Jesus seems to be referring to both His resurrection and ascension. At His death they would be sad. But at His resurrection their sorrow would turn into joy, for they would see Him again (verses 19–22).

But Jesus promises still more to the disciples. 'No one will take your joy from you' (verse 22). Even after the resurrection and ascension the disciples will continue to enjoy a personal relationship with Jesus Christ, and then they will understand more easily some of the more enigmatic sayings of Jesus which as yet they cannot grasp. The joy of that personal relationship will be fostered and will grow as they learn to have increasing confidence in prayer to the Father in the name of Jesus. Clearly, the coming of Jesus Christ into the world and His return to His Father is part of the Father's loving plan to deepen our relationship with Himself (verses 23, 24).

Jesus' clear claims to come from the Father and to return to Him strengthen the faith of the disciples (verses 29, 30). But He continues to warn them of their own moment of failure when they will all forsake Him and only His Father will remain faithful. Nevertheless, in their relationship with Jesus Christ there will be peace and joy and victory in the midst of trouble and difficulty. Jesus does not save us from tribulation, but He saves us *in* it. He gives us the strength to have victory in spite of it.

36 JESUS PRAYS FOR HIS DISCIPLES
17:1–19

1 When Jesus had spoken these words, he lifted up his eyes to heaven and said, 'Father, the hour has come; glorify thy Son that the Son may glorify thee, ²since thou hast given him power over all flesh, so that he might give eternal life to all whom thou hast given him. ³And this is eternal life, that they know thee the only true God, and Jesus Christ whom thou hast sent. ⁴I glorified thee on earth, having accomplished the work which thou gavest me to do; ⁵and now, Father, glorify thou me in thy own presence with the glory which I had with thee before the world was made.

6 'I have manifested thy name to the men whom thou gavest me out of the world; thine they were, and thou gavest them to me, and they have kept thy word. ⁷Now they know that everything that thou hast given me is from thee; ⁸for I have given them the words which thou gavest me, and they have received

**them and know in truth that I came from thee; and they have
believed that thou didst send me. ⁹I am praying for them; I
am not praying for the world but for those whom thou hast
given me, for they are thine; ¹⁰all mine are thine, and thine are
mine, and I am glorified in them. ¹¹And now I am no more in
the world, but they are in the world, and I am coming to thee.
Holy Father, keep them in thy name which thou hast given me,
that they may be one, even as we are one. ¹²While I was with
them, I kept them in thy name which thou hast given me;
I have guarded them, and none of them is lost but the son of
perdition, that the scripture might be fulfilled. ¹³But now I am
coming to thee; and these things I speak in the world, that they
may have my joy fulfilled in themselves. ¹⁴I have given them
thy word; and the world has hated them because they are not
of the world, even as I am not of the world. ¹⁵I do not pray that
thou shouldst take them out of the world, but that thou shouldst
keep them from the evil one. ¹⁶They are not of the world, even
as I am not of the world. ¹⁷Sanctify them in the truth; thy word
is truth. ¹⁸As thou didst send me into the world, so I have sent
them into the world. ¹⁹And for their sake I consecrate myself,
that they also may be consecrated in truth.'**

There are a number of references in the Gospels to Jesus praying.
We read that He prayed all night before He chose the disciples
(Luke 6:12). We read that He was praying when the disciples came
to ask Him to teach them to pray, and He gave them the model
prayer which we call the Lord's Prayer (Luke 11:1). He prayed in
the wilderness before He began His public ministry (Matthew 4;
Luke 4) and in the Garden of Gethsemane before He was arrested
and crucified (Matthew 26:36–44). But here in John's Gospel we
have the only account of a long prayer by Jesus. We have seen
that Jesus had a unique relationship to His Father. In sharing with
us an intimate moment in that relationship, we learn something of
the deep concerns of His heart for Himself and for His disciples.

Sometimes this prayer is called 'the high priestly prayer' because
in the Old Testament the high priest would go once a year into the
Holiest of Holies and pray for the people before he offered a sacrifice for their sins. So Jesus prays, before He lays down His own life
as a sacrifice for the sins of the whole world.

The prayer divides naturally into three sections: (a) A prayer
concerning His own mission (verses 1–5); (b) a prayer for the
eleven disciples (verses 6–19); (c) a prayer for those who would

believe in Christ through the teaching of the disciples—that is, a prayer for the church throughout all ages (verses 20–26).

a. A prayer for Himself (verses 1–5)

This is expressed in the words, 'Glorify thy Son that the Son may glorify thee.' Jesus knows that God's moment has come, 'the hour' to which all the ministry of Jesus has been moving. The climax of His life-work is upon Him. It will be a moment of glory for Jesus and His heavenly Father. That is what He confidently prays for. He has glorified God by His obedience to God's will, and now in accomplishing the work which God had given Him to do, He could already say 'I glorified thee on earth'.

Stop and think for a moment. In what way do you think Jesus most honoured God? By His matchless teaching? 'No man ever spoke like this man!' By His miraculous signs? 'Surely God was with Him' in those. Yet, astonishingly, the hour of glory is clearly *His death*. It was by His death that He made possible eternal life. It is by knowing God and Jesus Christ as Sin-bearer, Saviour and King, that we enjoy eternal life.

Of course the death of Jesus Christ is only the moment of glory because it led on to the resurrection and ascension. The resurrection demonstrated God's acceptance of the death of Christ as a sufficient sacrifice for sins. So Jesus also prays that the Father would honour Him with the sharing of the Father's glory once more (verse 5).

b. A prayer for the disciples (verses 6–19)

We notice that when Jesus describes His disciples in this prayer, He does not regard them as men who had become camp-followers and only vaguely believed in Him. A disciple then, as a disciple now, knows what it is to have the name (the person and work) of God made clear to him. God is not a remote and impersonal power or 'an old man in the sky'. He is a heavenly Father revealed in flesh and blood in Jesus Christ. It is impossible to be a Christian unless in some measure God has revealed Himself to us in the Person of Jesus Christ. A disciple belongs to Christ. A disciple keeps God's word (so he must read it), for the very words of God have been given to us by Jesus (verse 8). The disciple has a definite view of Jesus Christ. He knows He is not merely a man. He comes from God, and the disciple believes God has sent Him (verse 8). Christian discipleship has nothing to do with vague beliefs about God. There are certain objective truths which a Christian must believe if He is to experience eternal life. Furthermore, a Christian disciple is not only someone who belongs to God but in whom in some measure the power and love of Jesus is exhibited. As Jesus put it, 'I am glorified in them' (verse 10).

c. What does Jesus pray for His disciples?

1. *Keep them in thy name which thou hast given me, that they may be one, even as we are one* (verse 11). Jesus was concerned that His disciples should be kept in *unity*; He was concerned that no-one should *fall away* (verse 12). (Judas was already judged and lost.) He was concerned that they should experience the joy of Jesus in all their circumstances (verse 13) and that they should be kept from the evil one (verse 15).

2. *Sanctify them in the truth* (verses 14–19). Christians are 'in the world' but not 'of the world' (verses 14, 15, 18). Furthermore, Jesus sends them into the world, and has consecrated Himself in obedience even unto death so that they might similarly dedicate themselves to the task of doing God's will in the world. How are Christians to be kept true to Christ in their involvement in the world? It is not easy. For we have to avoid two extremes. As Dr Leighton Ford has expressed it: the two extremes are 'isolation from the world and imitation of the world. God does not want us to be either holier-than-thou or worldlier-than-thou. He wants us to be like Jesus, who came into the world to save the world. And this demands an attitude both of separation from the world in its sin, and identification with the world in its need. Without separation—the difference Christ makes—we have an audience but nothing to say. Without identification, we have something to say but no audience.'*

So the only way for the Christian to walk wisely in such a

* Leighton Ford, *The Christian Persuader.*

situation is by being 'sanctified' in the truth, with mind and life moulded by the truth of the Bible and the example of Jesus.

37 JESUS PRAYS FOR THE CHURCH
17:20–26

20 'I do not pray for these only, but also for those who are to believe in me through their word, ²¹that they may all be one; even as thou, Father, art in me, and I in thee, that they also may be in us, so that the world may believe that thou hast sent me. ²²The glory which thou hast given me I have given to them, that they may be one even as we are one, ²³I in them and thou in me, that they may become perfectly one, so that the world may know that thou hast sent me and hast loved them even as thou hast loved me. ²⁴Father, I desire that they also, whom thou hast given me, may be with me where I am, to behold my glory which thou hast given me in thy love for me before the foundation of the world. ²⁵O righteous Father, the world has not known thee, but I have known thee; and these know that thou hast sent me. ²⁶I made known to them thy name, and I will make it known, that the love with which thou hast loved me may be in them, and I in them.'

The most moving moment in this prayer is when Jesus begins to pray for all those who would later come to believe in Him through the word of the disciples. In these words He prays for the church in the twentieth century as much as in the first. It seems as if Jesus knew well what would spoil the witness of the church more easily than anything else. In spite of the commands of Jesus that we love one another, only too often the church has been split and divided and disunited. So He prays for later generations of Christians, 'that they may all be one; even as thou, Father, art in me, and I in thee, that they also may be in us, so that the world may believe that thou hast sent me.'

The twentieth century has seen a growing concern among

Christians to get together and to demonstrate a visible unity to the world. It is important, therefore, that we note the kind of unity for which Christ prayed.

a. It was a unity of spirit

'That they may all be one; even as thou, Father, art in me, and I in thee . . . so that the world may believe that thou hast sent me.' The unity between Christians should be like the spiritual unity between God the Father and God the Son. Now this is possible only as we share in the glory of Christ—His living presence and power (verse 22). This is possible through the gift of the Holy Spirit which God gives to those who believe in Christ, as we have noticed in an earlier passage (14:16). So there is a spiritual unity between all Christians, between all those who possess the Spirit of Christ. We are then 'all one in Christ Jesus', and it is important that we recognize that fact. Different denominations cannot break that unity. The church is an organism, not an organization, and all those 'in Christ' are in the *one* family.

If, then, there is already a spiritual unity between Christians, for what is Jesus praying? The answer lies in verse 23. Jesus prays that Christians may become '*perfectly* one'. Writing to the Christians at Ephesus, Paul exhorted them to be 'eager to maintain the unity of the Spirit in the bond of peace' (Ephesians 4:3). A spiritual unity between real Christians is already there, but it needs to be recognized, maintained and wherever possible *visibly* demonstrated, so that the world may know that the coming of Jesus Christ has really broken down man-made barriers. 'I will not believe in the Redeemer of these Christians', said Nietzsche, 'until I see that they are redeemed.' Paul gives a wonderful picture of Christians growing together in love and friendship with one another and with Christ, exercising their gifts for the good of the church and the glory of God, growing 'to the measure of the stature of the fullness of Christ' (Ephesians 4:13). Perfect love and unity will of course be fully achieved only when we share in the glory of Christ in heaven. Jesus prays that we may enjoy that experience one day, and promises until then a progressively deeper revelation and experience of the love of God in our lives (verses 24, 25). It is 'Christ in us' (verse 26) which is the basis of our spiritual unity with other Christians. This is something that all Christians can experience.

b. It was a unity of truth (verses 6, 8, 17–26)

Why is work towards visible unity in the church so slow and difficult? Undoubtedly it is partly a lack of love between Christians. It is also, and this is much more difficult, disagreement about the essential truths upon which Jesus clearly assumed that we would be united when He prayed that we might become perfectly one. The words of Paul again confirm the teaching of Jesus in this prayer. We are not to be like children 'tossed to and fro and carried about with every wind of doctrine . . . Rather, *speaking the truth* in love, we are to grow up in every way into him who is the head, into Christ . . .' (see Ephesians 4:14–16). The church of Jesus Christ is not only built on love, but upon the foundation of the apostles and prophets and Jesus Christ, the chief corner-stone (Ephesians 2:20). Unity must therefore be based upon the truth of Christ and His apostles. Jesus confirms this when He prays that the disciples might be *consecrated in the truth*, and adds '*thy word is truth*' (verse 17). He has already stated that the disciples have kept God's word (verse 6) and received the words of Christ as God's words, and that they know *in truth* that Jesus comes from God. There can be no real unity therefore if a fellow-Christian denies that Jesus comes from God, or claims that His teaching is not authoritative. That is why there is a place for contending for the truth of the gospel in the church of God. But if God calls us to do this, we must 'speak the truth in love'. The old maxim is still helpful today in these matters: 'In necessary things, unity; in doubtful things, liberty; in all things, charity.'

1 When Jesus had spoken these words, he went forth with his disciples across the Kidron valley, where there was a garden, which he and his disciples entered. ²Now Judas, who betrayed him, also knew the place; for Jesus often met there with his disciples. ³So Judas, procuring a band of soldiers and some officers from the chief priests and the Pharisees, went there with lanterns and torches and weapons. ⁴Then Jesus, knowing all that was to befall him, came forward and said to them, 'Whom do you seek?' ⁵They answered him, 'Jesus of Nazareth.' Jesus said to them, 'I am he.' Judas, who betrayed him, was standing with them. ⁶When he said to them, 'I am he,' they drew back and fell to the ground. ⁷Again he asked them, 'Whom do you seek?' And they said, 'Jesus of Nazareth.' ⁸Jesus answered, 'I told you that I am he; so, if you seek me, let these men go.' ⁹This was to fulfil the word which he had spoken, 'Of those whom thou gavest me I lost not one.' ¹⁰Then Simon Peter, having a sword, drew it and struck the high priest's slave and cut off his right ear. The slave's name was Malchus. ¹¹Jesus said to Peter, 'Put your sword into its sheath; shall I not drink the cup which the Father has given me?'

The garden, just across the Kidron Valley, was a favourite meeting-place for Jesus and His disciples. Quiet, secluded and restful, it was called the Garden of Gethsemane (Mark 14:32). Gethsemane means oil-press. Here oil would be extracted from the olives which grew on the slopes of the Mount of Olives. It is possible that the garden belonged to a well-to-do person in the city, who allowed Jesus and His disciples to use it from time to time.

According to the other Gospels Jesus spent some time praying in the garden that evening, while His disciples, worn out by the emotional excitement of the preceding hours, fell fast asleep. They were rudely awakened by the shining of torches and the clatter of weapons. Judas had betrayed his Master. How little Judas understood Jesus! Was it necessary to bring torches, when the Passover new moon shone so brightly? Did Judas really think he needed not only the Temple police ('officers') but a *speira* (band) of soldiers as well, which could mean as many as 200–600 men? The world has always overestimated the strength of force of arms.

It is at this point that we are very much aware that we are following an eyewitness account. The mention of officers as well as soldiers; the careful description of Jesus' conversation with these men (verses 4–8); the mention of Malchus by name (verse 10): even the careful note that it was the *right* ear which was affected by Peter's blow (verse 10). But as well as these factual details there were two interesting contrasts outlined here.

We have already noticed *the treachery of Judas* (see chapter 13). This is contrasted here with *the majesty of Jesus*. Jesus is the master of this situation, not Judas. It is Jesus who takes the initiative and steps forward to reveal His identity. It is Jesus whose words, 'I am he' (the divine name), and whose manner caused the soldiers to fall to the ground. How puny man is before Jesus Christ! These men came brandishing their weapons, confident in their resources, cocksure about success. 'We'll soon silence this crazy preacher with his hopeless idealism,' they seem to say. Then a look. A word. The divine name; and they shrink from His presence, afraid to lift a finger to touch Him. We sometimes swagger into Christ's presence like that. We come to demolish Him with our clever arguments. We come to put Him where we want Him, out of the way, locked up. He is too disturbing. But if we really met Him we too would fall to the ground. We would learn that no man could take His life from Him. He laid it down of His own free will.

The second contrast is between Jesus and Peter, and it reveals again *the impulsiveness of Peter* contrasted with *the steadiness of Jesus*. Peter makes a brave but misguided attempt to resist the arrest of his Master (verse 10). But it shows us only too clearly that he still has not understood that Jesus must suffer. Jesus, on the other hand, steadily moves to His death, determined to fulfil the promises of God (verse 9) and to do the will of God (verse 11). The cup which Jesus must drink is the cup of suffering. Sometimes in the Old Testament the prophets refer to the cup of God's wrath and judgment upon sin (see Isaiah 51:17, 22). In a real sense Jesus knew He must drink such a cup if man is to be saved from the judgment he deserves. In full knowledge of what He was doing, Jesus majestically and steadily moves forward to the cross.

39 JESUS IS TRIED BY THE ECCLESIASTICAL LEADERS
18:12–27

12 So the band of soldiers and their captain and the officers of the Jews seized Jesus and bound him. [13]First they led him to Annas; for he was the father-in-law of Caiaphas, who was high priest that year. [14]It was Caiaphas who had given counsel to the Jews that it was expedient that one man should die for the people.

15 Simon Peter followed Jesus, and so did another disciple. As this disciple was known to the high priest, he entered the court of the high priest along with Jesus, [16]while Peter stood outside at the door. So the other disciple, who was known to the high priest, went out and spoke to the maid who kept the door, and brought Peter in. [17]The maid who kept the door said to Peter, 'Are not you also one of this man's disciples?' He said, 'I am not.' [18]Now the servants and officers had made a charcoal fire, because it was cold, and they were standing and warming themselves; Peter also was with them, standing and warming himself.

19 The high priest then questioned Jesus about his disciples and his teaching. [20]Jesus answered him, 'I have spoken openly to the world; I have always taught in synagogues and in the temple, where all Jews come together; I have said nothing secretly. [21]Why do you ask me? Ask those who have heard me, what I said to them; they know what I said.' [22]When he had said this, one of the officers standing by struck Jesus with his hand, saying, 'Is that how you answer the high priest?' [23]Jesus answered him, 'If I have spoken wrongly, bear witness to the wrong; but if I have spoken rightly, why do you strike me?' [24]Annas then sent him bound to Caiaphas the high priest.

25 Now Simon Peter was standing and warming himself. They said to him, 'Are not you also one of his disciples?' He denied it and said, 'I am not.' [26]One of the servants of the high

priest, a kinsman of the man whose ear Peter had cut off, asked, 'Did I not see you in the garden with him ?' [27]**Peter again denied it; and at once the cock crew.**

The Temple police and the Roman soldiers bind Jesus, as Judas looks on, and take Him to the residence of the high priest, the Archbishop of Canterbury of the day. First, Jesus is brought to Annas, who had been high priest from AD 6 to 15, and was now high priest emeritus (verse 13). Later He is taken to Caiaphas (possibly in another room in the same house), who is the son-in-law of Annas, and the high priest at the time (verse 24). It was Caiaphas, John reminds us, who had callously said: 'It is expedient that one man should die for the people.' The high priests under the Romans were always more concerned with expediency than principle. They were the arch-collaborators with the hated enemy, Rome. The office of high priest was a matter of intrigue and bribery. The fact that four of the sons of Annas became high priest and that Caiaphas was his son-in-law speaks for itself.

At the same time that Jesus was being questioned, Simon Peter was able to use the influence of a friend, another disciple, to gain admittance to the servants' quarters of the high priest's residence. The trial of Jesus and Peter's denial take place at the same time. As Jesus calmly and majestically moves forward to His 'hour' of destiny, we notice both injustice and inconsistency towards Him.

a. Injustice (verses 19–24)

There is no doubt that the so-called trial by Annas and Caiaphas was thoroughly rigged. In Jewish law a prisoner could be condemned only by witnesses. That is why Jesus refuses to answer the high priest's questions (verse 19), and insists that He has spoken clearly enough on a number of public occasions for witnesses to give their evidence. The other Gospels make it clear that when Caiaphas produced witnesses to speak against Jesus, even though they were 'planted' to discredit Jesus, they still could not agree (Mark 14:53–59). The action of one of the Temple police (verse 22) is only too typical of those who have already made up their mind about Jesus, and who do not care for truth or justice. A brainwashing session in a totalitarian state is not far removed from this scene. Jesus understands only too well those who suffer injustice at the hands of unscrupulous men.

There is a passage in the Jewish Talmud which reads: 'Woe to the house of Annas: woe to their serpents hiss: they are High Priests: their sons are keepers of the treasury: their sons-in-law are guardians of the Temple and their servants beat the people with staves.' Annas was as notorious as he was unscrupulous. He and his family had made a pile of money. The Temple stalls which Jesus overturned because of the shameful exploitation of the poor were probably part of what was called 'the bazaars of Annas'. Jesus therefore had attacked the vested interests of Annas. When a man's financial interests are affected, he is sometimes only too ready to resist truth and to stoop to injustice.

b. Inconsistency (verses 15–18, 25–27)

If there is injustice among the enemies of Jesus, there is also inconsistency and failure among His friends. The other disciples have already deserted Jesus. Peter at least has the courage to stay as near as he can. But Peter now finds himself cut off from his friends and open to the curiosity, ridicule and possible hostility of the world. The words of the waitress, 'Are not you also one of this man's disciples?' could read, 'Surely *you* are not another of this man's disciples?' It is not easy to remain loyal to Christ in such situations. Peter had boasted so much, but was as weak as any of us when he was tested. Twice more he was questioned. Each time he denied that he belonged to Jesus, the other Gospels recording that he did this with oaths and curses (see Mark 14:71).

If we wonder how Peter could be so inconsistent, perhaps the other Gospels give us the clue. In the Garden of Gethsemane Jesus had encouraged the disciples to 'watch and pray' in readiness for the hours of crisis which were before them. Peter like the others slept rather than prayed. Jesus understands. 'The spirit indeed is willing, but the flesh is weak' (Mark 14:38). But there is no short cut to consistent Christian living. As Richard Trench expressed it:

'Lord, what a change within us one short hour
Spent in Thy presence will avail to make!

What heavy burdens from our bosoms take!
What parched ground refresh us with a shower!
We kneel, how weak! We rise, how full of power!
Why therefore should we do ourselves this wrong
Or others, that we are not always strong,
That we are sometimes overborne with care,
That we should ever weak or heartless be,
Anxious or troubled—when with us is prayer
And joy and strength and courage are with Thee?'

40 JESUS IS BROUGHT BEFORE THE ROMAN GOVERNOR-GENERAL
18:28–19:16

28 Then they led Jesus from the house of Caiaphas to the praetorium. It was early. They themselves did not enter the praetorium, so that they might not be defiled, but might eat the passover. ²⁹So Pilate went out to them and said, 'What accusation do you bring against this man?' ³⁰They answered him, 'If this man were not an evil-doer, we would not have handed him over.' ³¹Pilate said to them, 'Take him yourselves and judge him by your own law.' The Jews said to him, 'It is not lawful for us to put any man to death.' ³²This was to fulfil the word which Jesus had spoken to show by what death he was to die.

33 Pilate entered the praetorium again and called Jesus, and said to him, 'Are you the King of the Jews?' ³⁴Jesus answered, 'Do you say this of your own accord, or did others say it to you about me?' ³⁵Pilate answered, 'Am I a Jew? Your own nation and the chief priests have handed you over to me; what have you done?' ³⁶Jesus answered, 'My kingship is not of this world; if my kingship were of this world, my servants would fight, that I might not be handed over to the Jews; but my kingship is not from the world.' ³⁷Pilate said to him, 'So you are a king?' Jesus answered, 'You say that I am a king. For this I was born, and for this I have come into the world, to bear

witness to the truth. Every one who is of the truth hears my voice.' ³⁸Pilate said to him, 'What is truth?'

After he had said this, he went out to the Jews again, and told them, 'I find no crime in him. ³⁹But you have a custom that I should release one man for you at the Passover; will you have me release for you the King of the Jews?' ⁴⁰They cried out again, 'Not this man, but Barabbas!' Now Barabbas was a robber.

1 Then Pilate took Jesus and scourged him. ²And the soldiers plaited a crown of thorns, and put it on his head, and arrayed him in a purple robe; ³they came up to him, saying, 'Hail, King of the Jews!' and struck him with their hands. ⁴Pilate went out again, and said to them, 'Behold, I am bringing him out to you, that you may know that I find no crime in him.' ⁵So Jesus came out, wearing the crown of thorns and the purple robe. Pilate said to them, 'Here is the man!' ⁶When the chief priests and the officers saw him, they cried out, 'Crucify him, crucify him!' Pilate said to them, 'Take him yourselves and crucify him, for I find no crime in him.' ⁷The Jews answered him, 'We have a law, and by that law he ought to die, because he has made himself the Son of God.' ⁸When Pilate heard these words, he was the more afraid; ⁹he entered the praetorium again and said to Jesus, 'Where are you from?' But Jesus gave no answer. ¹⁰Pilate therefore said to him, 'You will not speak to me? Do you not know that I have power to release you, and power to crucify you?' ¹¹Jesus answered him, 'You would have no power over me unless it had been given you from above; therefore he who delivered me to you has the greater sin.'

12 Upon this Pilate sought to release him, but the Jews cried out, 'If you release this man, you are not Caesar's friend; every one who makes himself a king sets himself against Caesar.' ¹³When Pilate heard these words, he brought Jesus out and sat down on the judgment seat at a place called The Pavement, and in Hebrew, Gabbatha. ¹⁴Now it was the day of Preparation for the Passover; it was about the sixth hour. He said to the Jews, 'Here is your King!' ¹⁵They cried out, 'Away with him, away with him, crucify him!' Pilate said to them, 'Shall I crucify your King?' The chief priests answered, 'We have no king but Caesar.' ¹⁶Then he handed him over to them to be crucified.

Under the Roman occupation, the Jews had no legal right to put any man to death (verse 31). This was why they were prepared to call Pilate, the Roman governor in Jerusalem, in the small hours of the morning, to ratify their decision to sentence Jesus to death. In the plan of God this also strangely fulfilled Jesus' own insistence that He would be 'lifted up' to die (John 12:32). Jesus died on a cross not only 'at the hands of wicked men' but in 'the definite plan and foreknowledge of God' (Acts 2:23).

There is one further point to notice about the ecclesiastical leaders who handed Jesus over to Pilate. They were so blind and full of hatred for Jesus that they could see no inconsistency in carefully avoiding ceremonial defilement* (verse 28) and at the same time setting aside justice and truth, and planning a calculated political murder. Such is the awful plight of men, religious or otherwise, who 'strain out a gnat and swallow a camel' (Matthew 23:24), who make ritual more important than honesty in business, faithfulness in marriage, truthfulness in speech, love for their neighbour and openness to Jesus Christ and His truth.

The conversation between the Jews and Pilate shows that there was no love lost between them (verses 29–32; cf. John 18:35; 19:6, 12, 14–16, 20–22). Pilate must have been an able administrator to have been offered such a difficult job in the civil service of Rome. But history records that he handled the Jews in Palestine with little sympathy or understanding. He had nothing but contempt for them and was often cruel and brutal. Already the Jews in Palestine had threatened to report him to the Emperor Tiberius for his mishandling of civilian affairs. Pilate then was not too happy in his job or sure of his position. This may help us to understand the overwhelming impression in this story of the indecision of Pilate and, in contrast, the resolution of Jesus.

a. The indecision of Pilate

At first Pilate speaks contemptuously to Jesus. 'Are *you* (emphatic word in the Greek) the King of the Jews?' Clearly the Jews have dropped the charge of blasphemy in coming to Pilate, and concentrated on the supposed political offence. Jesus answers quietly

* The Jew believed that 'the dwelling places of Gentiles are unclean'. This was particularly true at Passover time when in a Gentile home leaven might be found, whereas it was banished from every Jewish home as part of the Passover festival (see Exodus 12:15, 18–20). Leaven was a symbol of wickedness and corruption.

and authoritatively (verses 34, 36) and explains that His kingdom is not of this world, and that He has come to witness to truth, not to reign by force. If Pilate cared about truth, he would acknowledge Jesus. Pilate's question 'What is truth?' might have been jesting or wistful. Certainly he knows Jesus is innocent (verse 38). But Pilate is like many of us. If truth is inconvenient and demands recognition and commitment, we hesitate.

Pilate hoped first that the Jews would make the decision for him and release Jesus (verses 39, 40). Then he compromised and arranged that Jesus should be flogged, hoping this would satisfy the Jews (verses 1-4). Flogging was severe and brutal. The back of Jesus would have been exposed to the lash of a long leather thong studded at intervals with pellets of lead and sharp pieces of bone. Few remained conscious under such treatment. Some died. Some went mad. In addition to this, there is the mocking of the soldiers (verse 3). The words 'Here is the man!' (verse 5) is clearly meant to arouse pity for the helpless victim.

But Pilate must still make a decision. 'Crucify him! Crucify him!' (verse 6). The crowds are stirred up by their leaders and are thirsty for His blood. Pilate still tries to avoid a decision. He is frightened, probably for superstitious reasons, when the Jews bring forward the blasphemy charge again (verse 7); but the real issue that settles the matter for Pilate is threat of the loss of his own personal position and standing as Governor. 'If you release this man, you are not Caesar's friend' (verse 12). Men today will still sell their soul because of fear of men, or fear that they will lose position or prestige. However much Pilate wanted 'to wash his hands' (see Matthew 27:24) of the whole affair, the moment came when he had to take sides for or against Christ. He tried feebly once more to get the Jews to make the decision for him (verses 14, 15). Then he handed Him over to them to be crucified.

There is one dramatic postscript to the trial that must have left Pilate cynical and astonished. When Pilate said 'Shall I crucify your King?' the chief priests, successors of those who acknowledged God as the only real King, could say, 'We have no king but Caesar.' Continued indecision and rejection of Jesus Christ leads not only to the abandonment of justice and truth, but of *God Himself.*

b. The resolution of Jesus

Here again we have one of the great contrasts in this Gospel. Pilate, weak and indecisive: Jesus, strong and resolute. It is clear that Pilate is far more 'on trial' than Jesus. It is Jesus, too, in spite of the flogging and the mocking, who has the greater authority. Only once in this narrative does Jesus refuse to answer one of Pilate's questions. Jesus always knows whether we really want to know the answer to our theological and intellectual questions. He once refused to answer Herod's questions (Luke 23:9). Jesus has no time for triflers, or those who show curiosity without concern. Pilate thought that he had the life of Jesus in his hands. Jesus knew that what authority Pilate had as Governor was given him by God. 'You would have no power over me unless it had been given you from above' (verse 11). In the knowledge that God was working out His purpose through Pilate and the chief priests and the Jews, Jesus, 'when he was reviled, . . . did not revile in return; when he suffered, he did not threaten; but he trusted to him who judges justly' (1 Peter 2:23).

We, too, stand on trial as we consider this story. There is real danger in continually trying to avoid making any decision about Jesus Christ. Anatole France, in the book *Mother of Pearl*, attempts to draw an imaginary picture of Pilate near the end of his life. He depicts him living in lust and luxury in a villa on the shores of Italy. Many years had passed when one day a visitor from Rome, conversing with him, said, 'By the way, Pilate, were you not a procurator in Judea when they put to death that man Jesus?' Pilate, looking at his visitor through bleary eyes, said, 'Jesus, Jesus, I don't remember the name!' This is an imaginary conversation without historical foundation. But it is true philosophically. We can even forget Jesus if we avoid His claims often enough.

17 So they took Jesus, and he went out, bearing his own cross, to the place called the place of a skull, which is called in Hebrew Golgotha. ¹⁸There they crucified him, and with him two others, one on either side, and Jesus between them. ¹⁹Pilate also wrote a title and put it on the cross; it read, 'Jesus of Nazareth, the King of the Jews.' ²⁰Many of the Jews read this title, for the place where Jesus was crucified was near the city; and it was written in Hebrew, in Latin, and in Greek. ²¹The chief priests of the Jews then said to Pilate, 'Do not write, "The King of the Jews," but, "This man said, I am King of the Jews." ²²Pilate answered, 'What I have written I have written.'

23 When the soldiers had crucified Jesus they took his garments and made four parts, one for each soldier. But his tunic was without seam, woven from top to bottom; ²⁴so they said to one another, 'Let us not tear it, but cast lots for it to see whose it shall be.' This was to fulfil the scripture,

'They parted my garments among them,
and for my clothing they cast lots.'

25 So the soldiers did this; but standing by the cross of Jesus were his mother, and his mother's sister, Mary the wife of Clopas, and Mary Magdalene. ²⁶When Jesus saw his mother, and the disciple whom he loved standing near, he said to his mother, 'Woman, behold your son!' ²⁷Then he said to the disciple, 'Behold your mother!' And from that hour the disciple took her to his own home.

28 After this Jesus, knowing that all was now finished, said (to fulfil the scripture), 'I thirst.' ²⁹A bowl full of sour wine stood there; so they put a sponge full of the wine on hyssop and held it to his mouth. ³⁰When Jesus had received the wine, he said, 'It is finished'; and he bowed his head and gave up his spirit.

It was about the sixth hour, according to John's reckoning, when Pilate passed the death sentence (verse 14). The Jewish custom was to reckon hours from 6 a.m. to 6 p.m. and 6 p.m. to 6 a.m. If John is consistent with Mark's Gospel, then he is probably following the western system of reckoning from midnight to noon and noon to midnight, a system which was in use in Asia Minor at the time this Gospel was written. So at 6 a.m. the death sentence was passed on Jesus. As was customary, Jesus began to carry His own cross, which, as the other Gospels tell us, proved too much for him. So Simon from Cyrene was press-ganged into carrying it for Him (see Matthew 27:32). Golgotha was possibly so named because it was a hill outside the city walls which was similar in shape to a skull. Calvary is the Latin name for it. The story is told with breathless simplicity and great restraint.

a. The meaning of His death

1. *His physical and mental sufferings.* John does not make much of this. 'There they crucified him, and with him two others, one on either side, and Jesus between them' (verse 17). Nothing could be more restrained. But we must remember that the horrors of crucifixion and the shame of such a death would be known well enough in the first century. Cicero talked about 'the most cruel and horrifying death' of crucifixion.

The shame of it may be seen in the fact that it was unthinkable that a Roman citizen should be crucified. Crucifixion was possible only for slaves and criminals. The Jew, for his part, believed that any man 'hanged on a tree' was under the 'curse of God' (see Deuteronomy 21:23; Galatians 3:13).

It is hard for us to imagine the physical pain and mental sorrow that Jesus suffered. Crucifixion followed the long periods of cross-questioning, the flogging with the Roman cat-o'-nine-tails, the insults, blows, spitting and scorn of His enemies, the desertion, betrayal, denial of many of His friends. Jesus, whose thoughts were always for others first (see verses 26, 27), gave no expression of His own physical and mental anguish until the main purpose for His death was finished (verse 28). Then, and not until then, He cried 'I thirst'. The scripture He fulfilled here was probably Psalm 69:21, 'for my thirst they gave me vinegar to drink.'

If God became man in Christ, then God is concerned about the physical and mental sufferings of mankind. A lady whom I was visiting, and who was enduring great suffering, found great comfort in being able to say sincerely, 'I could never have suffered more than He did.' Bishop Stephen Neill has written:* 'There are times when we are so afflicted by the suffering in the world that we are inclined to shake our fists at the sky, and blaspheme whatever God allows such things to happen in His world. If we are concerned about the hundreds of thousands of refugees, who are homeless and workless and rotting in the cheerless camps that are all that civilization has been able to provide for them, we may be inclined to say to Him, "What is the use of telling these people about you? You know nothing of what it is really like to be a refugee, and therefore you are not in a position to help them." To which He might well answer, "Did you never read that it is written, the Son of man hath not where to lay his head?" Or watching some helpless and cruel suffering, we might resentfully say, "Why do you permit such suffering that you do not share?" and we might not immediately catch His answer, "Well, have you ever tried being crucified?"'

2. *His spiritual sufferings.* There is no doubt, however, that the soul of His sufferings was the sufferings of His soul. John has made it clear that Jesus deliberately laid down His life to drink the cup of God's judgment upon sin (verse 11). It was in this way that God would be glorified. This was the purpose of the hour to which He had come. John also makes it clear that Jesus is doing this consciously and deliberately in order to fulfil the Old Testament prophecies which explain God's plan of suffering for sin. Jesus was indeed king, but His throne was a cross. He was king not only of the Jews but of the world, as the placard in Hebrew, Greek and Latin script, which Pilate cynically wrote, ironically suggested. The seamless robe (verse 24) which the soldiers cast lots for, just as the Old Testament had suggested (Psalm 22), might well have reminded John of the high priest's robe, without seam, and woven in one piece from top to bottom. For John's eye for symbolism would not fail to see that the great High Priest had now at last laid down His own life, a perfect sacrifice for sin, and had 'finished' (verse 30) the work which God had given Him to do.

'It is finished' is one word in the Greek. The other Gospels say that Jesus died with a great shout (Matthew 27:50; Mark 15:37; Luke 23:46). 'Finished' was a shout of triumph, not a cry of

* S. C. Neill, *Christian Faith Today*, p. 262.

resignation. It is left to the other Evangelists to describe the darkness, symbolic of the sin of the world which He bore in our place; Matthew speaks of the cry of desolation, 'My God, my God, why hast thou forsaken me?' It was this spiritual agony that was now *finished*. It was the bearing of the sin of the world, your sin and mine, coming as a cloud between the Father and the Son, which had to be endured and which was now *finished*. God's judgment had fallen. God had 'condemned sin in the flesh' of Jesus (Romans 8:3). God had 'laid on him the iniquity of us all' (Isaiah 53:6). 'God was in Christ reconciling the world to himself' (2 Corinthians 5:19). Jesus became 'a curse for us' that he might 'redeem us from the curse of the law' (Galatians 3:13). Jesus was the Lamb of God, taking away the sin of the world (John 1:29). He had now finished that great work. The Father was satisfied. It was the moment of glory. 'For God so loved the world that he gave his only Son, that whoever believes in him should not *perish*, but have eternal life' (John 3:16). He suffered judgment that we might escape judgment. He drank the cup of wrath that we might receive the cup of salvation. He died that we might live.

When the famous eighteenth-century preacher Charles Simeon was an undergraduate at King's College, Cambridge, he became conscious of his own lack of a real experience of forgiveness of sins and knowledge of God. He read a book in Passion week by a certain Bishop Wilson on the sacrifice of Christ. Simeon tells us, 'The thought came into my mind, What, may I transfer all my guilt to another? Has God provided an Offering for me, that I may lay my sins on His head? Then, God willing, I will not bear them on my own soul one moment longer. Accordingly I sought to lay my sins upon the sacred head of Jesus.'* That is what the cross makes possible. That is the basic meaning of the death of Christ.

b. The challenge of His death

It is impossible to remain neutral in the shadow of the cross. As John describes some of those who watched Him die we find three attitudes to Jesus and His sufferings which we still find today.

1. *Rejection*. There are no signs that the Jewish leaders are at all

* Handley C. G. Moule, *Charles Simeon*, pp. 25, 26.

repentant. They are furious that Pilate will not take down the placard 'Jesus of Nazareth, the King of the Jews'. Pilate is truculent. 'What I have written I have written' (verse 22). It is strange that he is so firm here, and so weak when it comes to deciding about Jesus. The Jewish leaders have made their decision. They have rejected Jesus. Many in the crowd had weakly followed the party line (verse 15). It was outright rejection, and weak acquiescence to the majority view, which led to the murder of Jesus Christ.

2. *Indifference.* One of the other Evangelists records Jesus' prayer at the crucifixion: 'Father, forgive them; for they know not what they do' (Luke 23:34). The soldiers who nailed Jesus to the cross were in many respects ignorant of what they were doing. They were carrying out their duty in doing a very unpleasant task. But although, like Jesus, we can recognize their ignorance, it is hard to excuse their indifference. They gambled as He suffered. They stood at the feet of the Son of God, and simply passed another day without, it seems, a thought about Him.

Studdart Kennedy expressed the indifference of twentieth-century man when he wrote:

'When Jesus came to Golgotha, they hanged Him on a tree,
They drove great nails through hands and feet and made a calvary.
They crowned Him with a crown of thorns, red were His wounds and deep,
For those were crude and cruel days, and human flesh was cheap.

When Jesus came to Birmingham, they simply passed Him by,
They never hurt a hair of Him, they only let Him die.
For men had grown more tender, and they would not give Him pain,
They only just passed down the street, and left Him in the rain.'

3. *Loyalty.* Jesus mentions four women who remained loyal to Him through it all. John was with them, and that same day began to discover the fellowship and friendship that binds together those who are loyal to the Saviour of the world (verses 26, 27). What is your attitude to Jesus Christ?

31 Since it was the day of Preparation, in order to prevent the bodies from remaining on the cross on the sabbath (for that sabbath was a high day), the Jews asked Pilate that their legs might be broken, and that they might be taken away. ³²So the soldiers came and broke the legs of the first, and of the other who had been crucified with him; ³³but when they came to Jesus and saw that he was already dead, they did not break his legs. ³⁴But one of the soldiers pierced his side with a spear, and at once there came out blood and water. ³⁵He who saw it has borne witness—his testimony is true, and he knows that he tells the truth—that you also may believe. ³⁶For these things took place that the scripture might be fulfilled, 'Not a bone of him shall be broken.' ³⁷And again another scripture says, 'They shall look on him whom they have pierced.'

38 After this Joseph of Arimathea, who was a disciple of Jesus, but secretly, for fear of the Jews, asked Pilate that he might take away the body of Jesus; and Pilate gave him leave. So he came and took away his body. ³⁹Nicodemus also, who had at first come to him by night, came bringing a mixture of myrrh and aloes, about a hundred pounds' weight. ⁴⁰They took the body of Jesus, and bound it in linen cloths with the spices, as is the burial custom of the Jews. ⁴¹Now in the place where he was crucified there was a garden, and in the garden a new tomb where no one had ever been laid. ⁴²So because of the Jewish day of Preparation, as the tomb was close at hand, they laid Jesus there.

In the Old Testament the Jews have a law which says: 'If a man has committed a crime punishable by death and he is put to death, and you hang him on a tree, his body shall not remain all night upon the tree, but you shall bury him the same day, for a hanged man is accursed by God' (Deuteronomy 21:22, 23). The Romans often left their criminals to die on the cross for days, and then refused to bury them. But once again we find the Jews careful to keep the law in some respects (verse 31) while remaining blind to vital issues. It is not enough to be a correct, orthodox, religious enthusiast. Our attitude to Christ matters far more than our attitude to religion.

The rest of this chapter emphasizes five further truths about the death of Christ.

a. It was real (verses 32–34)

Considerable publicity has been given in recent days to a book by Dr. Hugh Schonfield* which asserts that Jesus did not die on the cross, but was so drugged that He was able to survive crucifixion and the tomb. So it is important to notice the witness of John that Jesus was certainly dead when the soldiers came; and the piercing of His side was further confirmation for any who might wonder. It is hard to believe that Nicodemus and Joseph, in handling the body of Jesus, would not be certain of this fact too.

b. It was costly (verses 35, 36)

When John solemnly records the evidence of the witness who saw blood and water come from the pierced side of Jesus, it is clear that he regards this phenomenon as highly significant. In 1862 Sir James Simpson, writing from a medical point of view on the causes of the death of Christ, tried to account for the blood and water by suggesting that it was the sign of a ruptured heart. The blood of the heart mingled with the fluid of the pericardium which surrounds the heart. The spear pierced the pericardium and the mingled fluid and blood came forth. He believed that Jesus had died of a broken heart. More recent medical knowledge tends to support the view that the spear had drawn water from a dilated stomach as well as blood from the heart.† This too could have been due to His distress in the garden, and the sufferings of mind and soul.‡

Certainly His death was no ordinary death. It was costly. It involved the crushing sorrow of bearing the sin of the world.

* H. J. Schonfield, *The Passover Plot*.
† See R. V. G. Tasker, *The Gospel according to St. John*, pp. 212, 213.
‡ A. Rendle Short, *The Bible and Modern Medicine*, chapter 9 on 'The physical cause of the death of Christ'.

c. It was life-giving (verse 34)

It is hard to believe that John did not see symbolism in the blood and water. The blood speaks of the forgiveness made possible by the death of Christ. An early Jewish Christian wrote, 'Without the shedding of blood there is no forgiveness of sins' (Hebrews 9:22). The water usually signifies in John the new life (see John 4:14; 7:38, 39). God offers us, on the grounds of the death of Christ, forgiveness and new life.

d. It was planned (verse 36)

John is quick to point out that, even in the small incidents connected with the death of Christ, God's hand is seen in it all: 'For these things took place that the scripture might be fulfilled.'

e. It was powerful (verses 38–42)

The death of Jesus Christ is already beginning to exercise its power in drawing men out to acknowledge Him. Joseph of Arimathea and Nicodemus (see John 3) were two influential men in the Jewish Council, or Sanhedrin, who up to this point had remained as secret disciples. The fear of men had kept them from making known their secret allegiance to Jesus. But the death of Christ moves them not only to identify themselves with His cause, but to express generous though belated love for Jesus. Joseph unashamedly asks Pilate for permission to take away the body of Jesus (verse 38). Nicodemus, known for his retiring nature, brings vast quantities of costly spices for the burial (verse 39). Together they take the body down and bind it in the traditional way with linen cloths, placing the spices in between (verse 40). The tomb was a new tomb in a garden. Before the sabbath came they had reverently and lovingly laid the body of Jesus in the tomb and sealed up the entrance with a boulder (Mark 15:46).

The death of Jesus Christ still has power to call people from their fears and from their half-heartedness to unashamed service. C. T. Studd said about a turning-point in his own life: 'When I came to see that Jesus Christ had died for me, it didn't seem hard to give up all for him. It seemed just common, ordinary, honesty.'*

* Norman P. Grubb, *C. T. Studd: Cricketer and Pioneer*.

1 Now on the first day of the week Mary Magdalene came to the tomb early, while it was still dark, and saw that the stone had been taken away from the tomb. ²So she ran, and went to Simon Peter and the other disciple, the one whom Jesus loved, and said to them, 'They have taken the Lord out of the tomb, and we do not know where they have laid him.' ³Peter then came out with the other disciple, and they went toward the tomb. ⁴They both ran, but the other disciple outran Peter and reached the tomb first; ⁵and stooping to look in, he saw the linen cloths lying there, but he did not go in. ⁶Then Simon Peter came, following him, and he went into the tomb; he saw the linen cloths lying, ⁷and the napkin, which had been on his head, not lying with the linen cloths but rolled up in a place by itself. ⁸Then the other disciple, who reached the tomb first, also went in, and he saw and believed; ⁹for as yet they did not know the scripture, that he must rise from the dead. ¹⁰Then the disciples went back to their homes.

Mary Magdalene, who had stayed close to Jesus during the last hours of His life, came very early on Sunday morning to the garden tomb where they had buried Him. She was astonished to find that the heavy boulder, which had been placed in a groove and rolled in front of the entrance to the burial cave, had been rolled away. Hurriedly she fetched Peter and John, who came to examine the tomb and find out what had happened. John came to the conclusion that morning that Jesus was not dead but risen (verse 8). Clearly he did not expect such an astonishing event, and he had not understood that the Scriptures had foretold that the Messiah would rise again (verse 9). Later, in the preaching of the early Christians, the words from Psalm 16:10 were often quoted. The way the apostle Peter expounded this was as follows: 'David . . . foresaw and spoke of the resurrection of the Christ, that he was not abandoned to Hades, nor did his flesh see corruption' (Acts 2:25–

31). On that morning, however, it was other evidence that convinced John. *He saw and believed.*

When the young lawyer, Frank Morison, decided to write a book to disprove the resurrection of Jesus Christ, he said this about his own attitude to Christianity: 'As a young man,' he tells us, 'when I first began seriously to study the life of Christ, I did so with a very definite feeling that, if I may so put it, His history rested upon very insecure foundations.' However, as he began to study critically all the evidence on the last seven days of the life of Jesus before His crucifixion, he discovered that 'slowly but very definitely the conviction grew that the drama of those unforgettable weeks of human history was stranger and deeper than it seemed'. In the end Frank Morison was compelled to write one of the best books ever written on the evidence for the resurrection.* The book that he originally intended to write became 'the book that was never written'. Convinced by the cumulative evidence of the New Testament records, he argued instead for the truth of the resurrection of Jesus Christ. In the early eighteenth century a man called Gilbert West also determined to expose Christianity, but after a year's study he wrote, 'I have found the resurrection of Jesus Christ to be a true fact, and I too have become a believer, and have written my book on that side.' On the title page of his book, called *Observations on the History and Evidences of the Resurrection of Jesus Christ*, he had written the text, 'Blame not before thou hast examined the truth: understand first and then rebuke.'

We can examine here only the evidence of this one Gospel. What did John see that enabled him to believe that Jesus is risen? We notice in this passage two lines of evidence.

a. The empty tomb (verses 1, 2)

We must not isolate this evidence from the rest (see the next section, verses 11–31); but John certainly attaches importance to it. Later, when the Christians preached the resurrection, they knew that anyone could check up on this claim. The tomb was only a short distance from where they were preaching. Indeed the very

* Frank Morison, *Who moved the stone?*

fact that a rumour was spread that the disciples had stolen the body of Jesus at least emphasizes that the tomb *was* empty.

It is hard to believe that *the disciples stole the body*, because they would have no motive for doing so. It is not easy to believe that men would preach a doctrine which resulted in unpopularity with the authorities, persecution and even death, when they knew all the time that Jesus was not risen from the dead at all.

Some have argued that *His enemies stole the body*. Why did they not produce evidence of this when they tried to forbid the preaching of the early Christians? Others have said that *Jesus did not really die at all* (see above, p. 175). Long ago the historian, Strauss, answered this theory by saying, 'It is impossible that a being who had stolen half dead out of the sepulchre, who crept about weak and ill, wanting medical treatment, who required bandaging, strengthening and indulgence, and who still at last yielded to His sufferings, could have given the disciples the impression that He was a conqueror over death and the grave, the Prince of Life: an impression which lay at the bottom of their future ministry. Such a resuscitation could by no possibility have changed their sorrow into enthusiasm, have elevated their reverence into worship.' Furthermore, of course, on this explanation, Jesus Himself would be party to dishonesty and deception.

John saw an empty tomb, and believed that Jesus had risen.

b. The grave-clothes (verses 4–8)

Strictly speaking the tomb was not completely empty. The body of Jesus was no longer there, but the grave-clothes were so placed that John saw these—and believed. The significance of the grave-clothes is that John describes them as 'lying undisturbed'. That is the force of the Greek word (*keimena*) in verse 5. 'Lying collapsed' is one translation. The heavy spices placed between the folds would collapse the burial cloths once the body had gone, but the cloths remained intact. Furthermore, the napkin, or turban head-cloth, was still 'rolled up' (verse 7) or 'twirled' (*entetuligmenon*). It kept its turban shape and was lying exactly where the head of Jesus would have been.*

* For further reading see Michael Green, *Man Alive!*, especially pp. 41, 42.

On this evidence, it is clear that no-one could have stolen the body and left the grave-cloths like that. It is equally clear that Jesus could not have swooned, only to recover, remove the grave-clothes and escape. John saw, and believed.

44 MORE EVIDENCE FOR THE RESURRECTION
20:11–31

11 But Mary stood weeping outside the tomb, and as she wept she stooped to look into the tomb; [12]and she saw two angels in white, sitting where the body of Jesus had lain, one at the head and one at the feet. [13]They said to her, 'Woman, why are you weeping?' She said to them, 'Because they have taken away my Lord, and I do not know where they have laid him.' [14]Saying this, she turned round and saw Jesus standing, but she did not know that it was Jesus. [15]Jesus said to her, 'Woman, why are you weeping? Whom do you seek?' Supposing him to be the gardener, she said to him, 'Sir, if you have carried him away, tell me where you have laid him, and I will take him away.' [16]Jesus said to her, 'Mary.' She turned and said to him in Hebrew, 'Rabboni!' (which means Teacher). [17]Jesus said to her, 'Do not hold me, for I have not yet ascended to the Father; but go to my brethren and say to them, "I am ascending to my Father and your Father, to my God and your God."' [18]Mary Magdalene went and said to the disciples, 'I have seen the Lord'; and she told them that he had said these things to her.

19 On the evening of that day, the first day of the week, the doors being shut where the disciples were, for fear of the Jews, Jesus came and stood among them and said to them, 'Peace be with you.' [20]When he had said this, he showed them his hands and his side. Then the disciples were glad when they saw the Lord. [21]Jesus said to them again, 'Peace be with you. As the Father has sent me, even so I send you.' [22]And when he had said this, he breathed on them, and said to them, 'Receive

the Holy Spirit. ²³If you forgive the sins of any, they are forgiven; if you retain the sins of any, they are retained.'

24 Now Thomas, one of the twelve, called the Twin, was not with them when Jesus came. ²⁵So the other disciples told him, 'We have seen the Lord.' But he said to them, 'Unless I see in his hands the print of the nails, and place my finger in the mark of the nails, and place my hand in his side, I will not believe.'

26 Eight days later, his disciples were again in the house, and Thomas was with them. The doors were shut, but Jesus came and stood among them, and said, 'Peace be with you.' ²⁷Then he said to Thomas, 'Put your finger here, and see my hands; and put out your hand, and place it in my side; do not be faithless, but believing.' ²⁸Thomas answered him, 'My Lord and my God!' ²⁹Jesus said to him, 'Have you believed because you have seen me? Blessed are those who have not seen and yet believe.'

30 Now Jesus did many other signs in the presence of the disciples, which are not written in this book; ³¹but these are written that you may believe that Jesus is the Christ, the Son of God, and that believing you may have life in his name.

The two disciples returned to their homes, wondering. Mary remained by the tomb, weeping. Then in the midst of her sorrow the risen Lord came to her (verses 14–18). He came to the disciples in the upper room that same evening (verses 19–23). The following Sunday He came to the disciples again, this time when Thomas, who still doubted, was with them (verses 26–29). In these three dramatic stories the Evangelist emphasizes the reality and the effects of the resurrection appearances, which provides us with further evidence for the Christian claim that *Jesus is risen*.

a. The reality of the resurrection appearances

There is no doubt on the evidence here that the resurrection body of Jesus was real and not phantom. It was not identical with His earthly body, because it was not so limited. Jesus could appear among the disciples, even through closed doors (verse 19). He could appear and disappear at will, and in what must have been a startling manner. Furthermore, He obviously wanted to teach the disciples to depend less on His physical presence, and to prepare for a deeper and more spiritual relationship with Him. This would be possible once He had ascended to His Father. This must be the meaning of His words to Mary Magdalene, 'Do not hold me, for I have not yet ascended to the Father; but go to my brethren and say to them, "I am ascending to my Father and your Father, to my God and your God"' (verse 17). These words also emphasize the uniqueness of His own relationship to His Father. He does not say 'to *our* Father'; but 'to my Father and your Father'.

Nevertheless, although His risen body was different in some sense from His earthly body, it is clear that the disciples can recognize Jesus (verses 16, 20, 28). Mary could touch Him (verse 17). The disciples could see the marks of crucifixion in His hands and side (verse 20), and Thomas was invited to put his hands on them (verse 27). In the next chapter we read that Jesus could cook breakfast and eat it with the disciples (21:4-14). Jesus was no apparition.

Some have tried to explain away the appearances of Jesus as due to the disciples suffering hallucinations. Arnold Lunn describes an occasion when he himself suffered hallucinations when searching a mountain peak for the body of a friend of his who had been killed.* 'We had travelled all through the night from London, and started on our search party within an hour or two of arriving at the little inn from which he (the friend) started for his last climb. We were out of training and tired, and the strain of the search gradually began to tell. Every time we turned a corner *we expected to see our friend*; again and again we thought we saw his body stretched out on the rocks, and heard the other members of the party shouting that they had found him . . . These hallucinations were vivid while they lasted, *but they never lasted for more than a second or two.*'

If Lunn's experience of hallucinations is at all typical, then we see that the resurrection appearances do not fit the hallucination theory at all. The disciples of Jesus were certainly not *expecting* to see Jesus, risen from the dead. When Mary saw Jesus, she thought it was the gardener (verse 15). When the disciples in the upper room saw Jesus, we are told in Luke's Gospel that their first reaction was that 'they were startled and frightened, and supposed that they saw a spirit' (Luke 24:37). When Thomas was told by the others, 'We have seen the Lord,' he said, 'Unless I see in his

* Arnold Lunn, *The Third Day*, pp. 74, 75.

hands the print of the nails, and place my finger in the mark of the nails, and place my hand in his side, I will not' (in the Greek a double negative is used for emphasis: 'no never') 'believe' (verse 25). Furthermore, these appearances of Jesus clearly lasted for more than a few seconds, and far from the effects wearing off, the disciples became so convinced that Jesus was alive that they were prepared to suffer imprisonment, persecution and death rather than stop preaching the resurrection.

b. The effects of the resurrection appearances

Those who deny the resurrection of Jesus Christ have a difficult task to explain the changed lives of the disciples following the death of their Leader. John hints at the effects of the resurrection in this chapter.

1. *Sorrow is turned into joy* (verses 11–16). Mary is overcome with grief at the death of Jesus (verses 11, 15). She starts the day by saying bitterly, 'They have taken away my Lord, and I do not know where they have laid him.' She ends the day by joyfully telling the disciples, 'I have seen the Lord.' It is still true today that the Christian, who mourns the loss of a close relative or friend, can experience peace and joy in the knowledge of the risen Lord Jesus.

2. *Fear is turned into boldness* (verses 19–23). The disciples skulked behind locked doors 'for fear of the Jews', the Evangelist tells us. Their hopes and plans had been dashed to the ground by the death of Jesus. 'We had hoped that he was the one to redeem Israel', one of them said miserably (Luke 24:21).

Then Jesus came to them. He promised them peace instead of their fears (verses 19, 21) and power in place of their feebleness (verses 21 23). He would send them out into the world to bring the assurance of forgiveness to those who turned from their sins and trusted in the Lord Jesus Christ. 'As the Father has sent me, even so I send you.' Then He breathed on them, symbolically assuring them of the breath of God's Spirit who would come to them and strengthen them. A few weeks later these same men were witnessing with such boldness that thousands became Christians. They had such courage that they sang hymns in prison and prayed for their persecutors when stoned to death. It was said of these men that 'they could not but speak of the things they had seen and heard '(see Acts 4:20).

3. *Doubt is turned into faith* (verses 24–26). Thomas wanted proof (verse 25). A week went by, and then Thomas saw the risen Lord. Jesus gently rebuked him, but offered him the evidence he wanted. 'Put your finger here, and see my hands; and put out your hand, and place it in my side; do not be faithless, but believing.' Thomas's expression of personal faith and commitment comes as a climax to this Gospel, '*My* Lord and *my* God!'

When Jesus says 'Blessed are those who have not seen and yet believe', it is a word for us. This assurance of faith is possible for all those who personally trust Jesus as Lord and God. Malcolm Muggeridge has told how he was filming in the Holy Land, and walking with a friend along the same road, the Emmaus Road, that Jesus had walked with two disciples on that first Easter morning. 'As my friend and I walked along like Cleopas and his friend, we recalled as they did the events of the Crucifixion and its aftermath in the light of our utterly different and yet similar world. Nor was it a fancy that we too were joined by a third presence. And I tell you that wherever the walk, and whoever the wayfarers, there is always this third presence ready to emerge from the shadows and fall in step along the dusty, stony way.'* The risen Christ still turns doubt into faith.

'These are written that *you* may believe that Jesus is the Christ, the Son of God, and that believing you may have life in his name.'

* Malcolm Muggeridge, *Another King*, p. 14.

45 THE CHALLENGE OF CHRISTIAN DISCIPLESHIP

21 : 1–25

1 After this Jesus revealed himself again to the disciples by the Sea of Tiberias; and he revealed himself in this way. ²Simon Peter, Thomas called the Twin, Nathanael of Cana in Galilee, the sons of Zebedee, and two others of his disciples were together. ³Simon Peter said to them, 'I am going fishing.' They said to him, 'We will go with you.' They went out and got into the boat; but that night they caught nothing.

4 Just as day was breaking, Jesus stood on the beach; yet the disciples did not know that it was Jesus. ⁵Jesus said to them, 'Children, have you any fish?' They answered him, 'No.' ⁶He said to them, 'Cast the net on the right side of the boat, and you will find some.' So they cast it, and now they were not able to haul it in, for the quantity of fish. ⁷That disciple whom Jesus loved said to Peter, 'It is the Lord!' When Simon Peter heard that it was the Lord, he put on his clothes, for he was stripped for work, and sprang into the sea. ⁸But the other disciples came in the boat, dragging the net full of fish, for they were not far from the land, but about a hundred yards off.

9 When they got out on land, they saw a charcoal fire there, with fish lying on it, and bread. ¹⁰Jesus said to them, 'Bring some of the fish that you have just caught.' ¹¹So Simon Peter went aboard and hauled the net ashore, full of large fish, a hundred and fifty-three of them; and although there were so many, the net was not torn. ¹²Jesus said to them, 'Come and have breakfast.' Now none of the disciples dared ask him, 'Who are you?' They knew it was the Lord. ¹³Jesus came and took the bread and gave it to them, and so with the fish. ¹⁴This was now the third time that Jesus was revealed to the disciples after he was raised from the dead.

15 When they had finished breakfast, Jesus said to Simon Peter, 'Simon, son of John, do you love me more than these?' He said to him, 'Yes, Lord; you know that I love you.' He said to him, 'Feed my lambs.' ¹⁶A second time he said to him, 'Simon, son of John, do you love me?' He said to him, 'Yes, Lord; you know that I love you.' He said to him, 'Tend my sheep.' ¹⁷He said to him the third time, 'Simon, son of John,

do you love me?' Peter was grieved because he said to him the third time, 'Do you love me?' And he said to him, 'Lord, you know everything; you know that I love you.' Jesus said to him, 'Feed my sheep. [18]Truly, truly, I say to you, when you were young, you girded yourself and walked where you would; but when you are old, you will stretch out your hands, and another will gird you and carry you where you do not wish to go.' [19](This he said to show by what death he was to glorify God.) And after this, he said to him, 'Follow me.'

20 Peter turned and saw following them the disciple whom Jesus loved, who had lain close to his breast at the supper and had said, 'Lord, who is it that is going to betray you?' [21]When Peter saw him, he said to Jesus, 'Lord, what about this man?' [22]Jesus said to him, 'If it is my will that he remain until I come, what is that to you? Follow me!' [23]The saying spread abroad among the brethren that the disciple was not to die; yet Jesus did not say to him that he was not to die, but 'If it is my will that he remain until I come, what is that to you?'

24 This is the disciple who is bearing witness to these things, and who has written these things; and we know that his testimony is true.

25 But there are also many other things which Jesus did; were every one of them to be written, I suppose that the world itself could not contain the books that would be written.

This last chapter may have been added to deal with a rumour that John, 'the disciple whom Jesus loved', would remain alive until Jesus came again at the end of the world (verse 23). John carefully recounts the incident when the words which gave rise to this rumour were actually said. John himself writes down the conversation to correct a false impression (verse 24). His concern for sober truth is a characteristic of this Gospel.

But there is no doubt, too, that this third and last appearance of Jesus recorded in John's Gospel (verse 14) is a fitting climax to the story of Jesus, and to our own consideration of the claims and demands of Christian commitment in terms of obedience, love, service and discipleship.

a. Obedience

There is restlessness and perhaps impatience in the decision of Peter and some of the other disciples to go fishing (verse 3). The strain of recent events was no doubt beginning to tell. Maybe there was also a hankering for the old life. It was possibly an impulsive decision by Peter, which the others were only too glad to comply with. But, as so often happens to the Christian who acts impulsively, the fishing trip was a failure. That night they caught nothing (verse 3).

It was at this point of failure that Jesus once again revealed Himself to these disciples. After a cold, wet and miserable night the dawn broke and the fishermen saw a stranger standing on the seashore. The question 'Children, have you any fish?' is met with an emphatic and impatient 'No'. But when the stranger gives the authoritative command 'Cast the net on the right side of the boat, and you will find some', they not only obey and make a great catch, but John recognizes the stranger as Jesus.

Once again in a fishing incident (cf. Luke 5) Jesus has revealed Himself to the disciples. He has made it clear that obedience is better than impatience. If we want to become effective disciples of Jesus Christ we must also learn to wait and to listen and to obey Jesus. The net was full of large fish, and somebody even bothered to count them (verse 11). Indeed this comment by the writer, the description of Peter's impulsive rushing into the sea (verse 7), the careful noting that the net was full of fish and not broken, and that the boat was one hundred yards off the shore, are all evidences of an eyewitness account. When Jesus invites the disciples to bring some of the fish they have caught as a contribution to the breakfast He has begun to prepare for them (verses 9, 10), we catch a glimpse of the love of Jesus for those who obey Him. Sometimes He teaches us the importance of obedience in failure and difficult circumstances. But always He understands our human weakness, and cares for our physical as well as spiritual needs (verses 12, 13). He also demonstrates to the disciples that He is no ghost or spirit—but the living, risen Lord.

b. Love

Simon Peter had denied Jesus three times in the courtyard of the high priest (see John 19). According to Luke's Gospel, Jesus had met Peter privately after the resurrection and probably he was then assured of forgiveness (Luke 24:34). Now He gives Peter the opportunity to wipe out the threefold denial with a threefold affirmation of love and loyalty.

When Jesus says to Peter, 'Simon, son of John, do you love me *more than these?*' He may be referring to the other disciples or to his fishing-nets. Peter had often boasted of his love for Jesus (see Mark 14:29). Did he now really love Jesus more than these others? Was he learning humility with his love? Was his love for Christ stronger than his love for his fishing? Jesus requires us to love Him with all our heart and soul and mind and strength. Love for our job, or our family, or friends, or pleasures must never count more than our love for Him. Furthermore, love for Christ is the only motive that will keep the Christian disciple faithful to Christ whatever the circumstances. It is not enough to want to be successful, or to want to do good in the world, or to leave the world a better place. We can easily be disillusioned if that is our motive for Christian service. Jesus wants to make sure that we love Him.*

c. Service

The Christian disciple has been saved to serve. Jesus is here commissioning Peter for service, which He describes in the familiar terms of doing the work of a shepherd. Jesus had previously implied (see Luke 5:1–11) that Peter would become a fisher of men, an evangelist. He now calls him also to the work of a shepherd, a pastor to the church of God. His responsibility would be for the young (the lambs) and the older, maturer Christians (the sheep). The lambs must be fed with appropriate food (verse 16); the sheep must be cared for, watched over and fed.

The test of our love for Jesus Christ will be seen in our willingness to serve Him. He calls us to be fishers of men, seeking to

---

* Many commentators point out that two different Greek words are used for 'love'. In verses 16 and 17 the verb for love employed by Jesus is *agapaō*, which speaks of the highest kind of love, God's love (see John 3:16). When Peter answers he uses the word *phileō*, which implies friendship or fondness. In the third question Jesus uses Peter's own word (*phileō*), which challenged Peter's sincerity. That may be the reason for Peter's sorrow (verse 17). However, this may be reading too much into the text, as these words are used synonymously in this Gospel and if Jesus was speaking in Aramaic there are no such distinctions.

introduce our friends to Jesus Christ. He may well call some of us to be shepherds, caring for young Christians, teaching the message of the gospel, supporting and encouraging the weak. But many people ask, how can I know what God wants me to do, and how can I best serve Him? Jesus implies that He has a different plan for each of us, and our part is to follow Him.

d. Discipleship

For Peter this would mean a life-time of leadership in the Christian church, caring for the needs of God's people. It would not be an easy task, and as he grew older he would find himself more restricted (verse 18) and he would eventually die a martyr's death. Tradition tells us that Peter was crucified upside-down. Certainly Jesus indicated some such death; but the writer comments, 'This he said to show by what death he was to glorify God' (verse 19). A Christian may bring honour to God even in the way that he dies.

But not everyone is called by Christ to such a responsible task or to such a dramatic end. He has a different plan for each of us. Like Peter, we are often curious about God's plans for another person. When Peter notices John following them he says, 'Lord, what about this man?' The reply that Jesus makes helps us to understand the importance of personally following Jesus, and not encouraging curiosity or even jealousy about God's plans for others. 'If it is my will that he remain until I come, what is that to you? *Follow me!*'

In some ways John's life-work was less dramatic than Peter's. He became a man of reflection and deep thought, calling men and women in the pagan city of Ephesus to put their trust, not in vague religious experience or speculation, but in the historical Jesus. John must have lived to a very old age. Length of life is in God's hands.

Our task is to follow Jesus. He may call us to a position of responsibility or leadership in the church, or in business, or in one of the professions, or in industry, or in the local community or in the home. He may call us to stay at home or to go overseas. We follow Him as we read His words to us in the Bible and obey them. We follow Him as we talk to Him in prayer and trust Him to order the circumstances of our lives. For, as in the case of this Gospel, the witness of the Bible to God's dealings with men is a true witness (verse 24).

Much more could have been written in this Gospel and in the other Gospels (verse 25). But God has given us enough to know His will, so that we may follow Him all the days of our life.